CANADIAN MANAGERIAL ACCOUNTING CASES

Lynn Carty BA, CMA
Assistant Professor (Accounting)
University of Guelph

Sara Wick CPA, CA
Assistant Professor (Accounting)
University of Guelph

WILEY

Library and Archives Canada Cataloguing in Publication

Carty, Lynn, 1967-, author
   Canadian managerial accounting cases / Lynn Carty, BA, CMA, Assistant
Professor (Accounting), University of Guelph, Sara Wick, CPA, CA, Assistant
Professor (Accounting), University of Guelph.
ISBN 978-1-118-75723-9 (pbk.)
   1. Managerial accounting—Case studies.   I. Wick, Sara, 1981-, author
II. Title.
HF5657.4.C3595 2014   658.15'11   C2014-903723-6

Production Credits

Acquisitions Editor: Zoë Craig
Vice President and Publisher: Veronica Visentin
Director of Marketing: Joan Lewis-Milne
Marketing Manager: Anita Osborne
Editorial Manager: Karen Staudinger
Developmental Editor: Daleara Jamasji Hirjikaka
Editorial Assistant: Maureen Lau
Cover Design: Joanna Vieira
Cover Image: ©istock.com/Stacey Newman
Typesetting: Thomson Digital
Printing & Binding: Courier

Printed and bound in the United States of America

1 2 3 4 5 CC 19 18 17 16 15 14

John Wiley & Sons Canada, Ltd.
5353 Dundas Street West, Suite 400
Toronto, ON, M9B 6H8 Canada
Visit our website at: www.wiley.ca

ABOUT THE AUTHORS

Lynn Carty is an assistant professor in the Department of Management at the University of Guelph, where she teaches various undergraduate managerial and financial accounting courses. Lynn has also taught at Wilfrid Laurier University and in the Accelerated Program for the Society of Management Accountants of Ontario. Lynn is a Chartered Professional Accountant (CPA) and has an Honours Bachelor of Arts in economics (University of Waterloo). Before teaching, Lynn held a variety of senior roles in the financial services and insurance industries. This included manager of budgeting and expense management, mutual fund dealership accountant, and consultant in the development of an activity-based costing system.

Sara Wick is an assistant professor in the Department of Management at the University of Guelph. Sara teaches both managerial and financial accounting at the undergraduate level. Prior to lecturing at the University of Guelph, she held lecturing positions at Wilfrid Laurier University and at McMaster University. In addition to being a Chartered Professional Accountant (CPA), Sara has an Honours Bachelor of Arts in economics and accounting (Wilfrid Laurier University) and a Master of Business Administration (Schulich School of Business, York University). Sara worked at PricewaterhouseCoopers LLP in Waterloo, Ontario, while working toward her CPA designation.

ACKNOWLEDGEMENTS

The authors would like to thank the following individuals for their valuable contributions to *Canadian Managerial Accounting Cases:*

Sandy Kizan, Athabasca University
Amy Lunov, University of Regina
Mary Oxner, St. Francis Xavier University
Sandy Qu, York University
Jo-Anne Ryan, Laurentian University
Frank Saccucci, MacEwan University
Glen Stanger, Douglas College
Patricia Stringer, University of Alberta

The authors would like to thank the following reviewers for their valuable suggestions:

Amy Lunov, University of Regina

Winston Marcellin, George Brown College

Sheila McGillis, Laurentian University

The authors would also like to thank Ilene Gilborn, Associate Professor (retired), Mount Royal University, for her help in developing the instructor resources associated with this text.

INTRODUCTION

Managerial Accounting and Cases—A Natural Fit

Managerial accounting and cases are a natural fit from a learning perspective because managerial accounting is all about decision-making in an organization. Cases set the stage for the decision, providing both qualitative and quantitative information that students, or individuals from the case, need to analyze in order to make a decision.

Goal of this Casebook

The overall goal of this casebook is to help students gain a deep understanding of managerial accounting by applying managerial accounting tools to a variety of typical business decisions.

In addition, this book is a learning tool for students not available in typical managerial accounting textbooks. Textbooks focus on teaching students the theoretical concepts of managerial accounting and the mechanics of the various managerial accounting tools. Examples within chapters and end-of-chapter problems teach these tools and reinforce concepts. Sometimes, textbooks have case-type questions as part of their end-of-chapter material, but these are typically longer versions of the types of questions within the chapter. These case-type questions also tend to focus only on the topics in that chapter.

The authors have assembled a variety of cases that span the chapters and topics covered in most introductory or intermediate managerial accounting textbooks so that students have the opportunity to learn from cases throughout their managerial accounting course. While each case has a primary focus, such as cost-volume-profit analysis, some cases touch on multiple areas of managerial accounting to challenge students to think about all the course's topics that apply to the case, unlike most textbook cases. There is at least one case that focuses on each of the following topics:

- » corporate governance
- » cost classifications
- » job-order costing
- » process costing
- » activity-based costing
- » techniques for measuring fixed and variable costs
- » cost-volume-profit analysis (single- and multi-product situations)

> » variable costing
>
> » budgeting
>
> » variances (production and marketing variances)
>
> » performance measurement
>
> » relevant costs
>
> » capital budgeting

Analyzing Cases within a Managerial Accounting Framework

Some cases in this book give students specific direction about what is required to analyze the case (such as a series of questions or ideas about the approach to take with the case). Others are intentionally written with no specific direction or hints. This is intended to recreate a real-life decision-making situation as much as possible, where managers are faced with an issue (or issues) or a decision they need to make. For example, should they launch a new product? Should they purchase a new machine? Should they accept a special order from a one-time customer? In cases without any specific direction, students have the chance to think about the managerial accounting tools they have learned and decide which one(s) a manager would use in that situation. The goal is to promote a deeper type of learning where students will come to truly understand what the various managerial accounting tools are used for and how to use them in various settings, as well as the advantages and potential limitations of the tools for decision-making in organizations.

The following is a suggested framework for students when analyzing managerial accounting cases that could be applied to any of the cases in this book and will be used in the teaching notes for some of the non-directed cases. This framework is in line with the CPA method of analyzing cases and will be of special interest to instructors who wish to expose their students to this manner of case analysis.

Examination of the Facts

The first step in analyzing a case is filtering through all the information in the case. In doing this, you will be able to uncover the issue, identify any key success factors or constraints, and determine the alternatives.

Issue

This is the main problem(s) in the case. Often, there will be multiple issues and you will need to determine which one is most important based on the case facts. Sometimes there are secondary issues that need to be analyzed but they are not the main focus of the case. For example, a case could focus on capital budgeting and the issue is whether or not to purchase a new machine. Secondary issues could relate to how the company's performance evaluation system should be structured to encourage managers to make decisions in the best interest of the company, but this is not the main focus of the case.

You should be able to express the issue in the form of a question. For example, "Should the company purchase a new machine?" could be the issue.

Students often have trouble determining what the issue is, especially when first learning how to analyze cases. Expressing the issue in terms of a question will help you separate the issue from other facts in the case.

Keep an eye out for ethical issues in a case. Decisions that managers make can have a variety of ethical implications. For instance, issues related to product quality, estimating product costs, or designing performance evaluation systems could have ethical implications depending on the situation.

TIP: Most cases will ask you to assume the role of one of the individuals in the case. For example, you could be a manager in the organization, a new employee in the accounting department, or an outside consultant. Think of how you would approach analyzing the case if you were this individual.

TIP: Putting yourself in the role of one of the individuals in the case will help you to figure out if there are ethical issues involved. Think of who would benefit and who would be harmed by what is happening in the organization. (Don't forget about external stakeholders like customers.)

Key Success Factors and Constraints

In certain cases, there will be key success factors and constraints you need to deal with. Key success factors are like a simplified version of the organization's strategy. What does the organization need to do in order to be successful? For example, exceptional product quality and customer service or flexible manufacturing capabilities could be key success factors. These will be different for each case because they are specific to the unique strategy of each company. Constraints are things that place restrictions on the options and choices available to management. For example, there may be a short supply of a certain type of materials or labour hours may be restricted due to union rules.

TIP: Look at the qualitative facts in the case for clues to see if there are key success factors or constraints you need to include in your response to the case..

Alternatives

In most managerial accounting cases, there is a decision to be made that is identified as the issue. To analyze a case, you should then identify alternative courses of action the organization could take based on the issue. For example, the alternatives could be:

1. Purchase Machine A.
2. Purchase Machine B.
3. Keep the existing machine (do nothing).

TIP: Don't forget about the "do nothing" alternative. This should be analyzed as well if it is a viable option for the organization.

Analysis

One of the advantages of learning with cases is that you will be challenged to do both qualitative and quantitative analysis.

Qualitative Information

Each alternative should then be analyzed based on the qualitative facts in the case. Think of this as a list of pros and cons, or advantages and disadvantages. For example, Machine A may produce a higher-quality product than Machine B. Tied to the company's key success factor of providing exceptional product quality, this would be a reason to purchase Machine A over Machine B. Just like key success factors, the qualitative analysis will be different for each case that you do because it is specific to the facts of that case.

Also, qualitative analysis can include some of the advantages and disadvantages of the various managerial accounting tools you have learned about. For example, if the case is about whether to implement an activity-based costing system or to keep using a traditional costing system, then the qualitative analysis should include the benefits and drawbacks of each of these, which are that activity-based costing is more accurate but also more time-consuming than a traditional costing system.

TIP: Be careful not to restate quantitative facts in words. This is not qualitative analysis. For example, the fact that income is greater in Alternative 1 versus Alternative 2 is not qualitative analysis.

<u>Quantitative Information</u>

Each alternative should also be analyzed from a quantitative perspective. Here, you need to use the information given in the case to determine the appropriate managerial accounting tool to answer the question you gave as the issue. For example, a long-term decision to purchase a new machine would be treated from a capital budgeting perspective and you would calculate net present value. A short-term decision to accept a one-time special order from a new customer would use a relevant cost approach to calculate the incremental income from accepting the special order.

Deciding which tool to use in your casebook quantitative analysis is often challenging for students because you are not directly told what to do. With textbook problems, you know it's a capital budgeting question or a relevant costing question because the problems you work on directly relate to the chapter you are studying.

Some cases have uncertainty built into the quantitative analysis, which means you can do a "sensitivity analysis." For example, the case may say there is a chance the cost of direct materials will increase by 10%. Your quantitative analysis can then be recalculated based on this.

TIP: If you are not sure which tool to use, think of the chapters you have covered so far in the course and the different tools that were used to solve the types of problems facing managers in those chapters.

TIP: Don't feel you need to use every number that is given in the case. Remember that in managerial accounting, many costs are considered sunk or irrelevant to the decision.

TIP: Overhead is often given in total and this will not change if the number of units changes. You need to remember to split it into fixed and variable overhead so that you can keep the fixed portion constant and only change the variable portion.

Conclusion and Recommendation

After all of your analysis, don't forget to summarize your results in the form of a conclusion and make a recommendation. Your recommendation should answer the question you laid out as your issue. For example, you would state that the company should buy the new machine. This needs to be supported by your analysis of the issues from a qualitative and quantitative perspective, keeping in mind the organization's key success factors.

Your recommendation should also include suggestions about how the organization can overcome any challenges you predict with your recommendation. For example, you recommend that Machine A be purchased, but it requires highly specialized, scarce labour to operate. Your recommendation could deal with this by mentioning that management should create an action plan stating how they are going to find and hire the people they need to run the machine.

Students in the same class may have different recommendations, especially in cases where there is a lot of qualitative analysis that can be interpreted from different perspectives. Also, sometimes the qualitative analysis points to one alternative while the quantitative analysis points to another.

TIP: The challenges associated with your recommendation will be found in your list of disadvantages for the alternative you are recommending. Look at the disadvantages you identified. For example, the fact that Machine A needs highly specialized, scarce labour is a disadvantage of purchasing Machine A.

Overview

Think of a case like a puzzle and all of the pieces of the puzzle need to fit together. Your recommendation is the final piece of the puzzle in your case analysis that ties everything together.

TIP: You will be given a lot of information in a case that you need to organize and analyze. Think of this case framework as a way to help you do this.

TIP: Don't just repeat facts from the case. You need to use the facts given in the case and analyze them to help the organization make a decision.

Don't be intimidated by cases. Whether they give you specific direction about what you need to do, or they are completely open-ended, try to use what you know about managerial accounting to solve the problem the case presents. Learning managerial accounting with cases will help you to gain a deeper understanding of managerial accounting and sharpen your decision-making skills. By putting yourself in the role of one of the individuals in the case, you will have the chance to experience how managerial accounting is used as an invaluable tool to make decisions in different organizations.

TABLE OF CONTENTS

Chapter 1: Corporate Governance

1.1 RTTC Inc.

RTTC is a public company whose primary business is the sale of personal and business computers. RTTC has been in operation for over 30 years, but has operated as a public company only in the last three years. RTTC has a board of directors that is made up primarily of independent directors. The following is a list of the board members:

Leroy Michaels – Chair (non-independent director)

Joan Michaels – Director (Chair of the Audit Committee)

Sarah Tov Ly – Director (Chair of the Compensation Committee)

Janet Calpito – Director (Chair of the Finance Committee)

Pascal Chénier – Director

Colin Schmidt – Director

Trevor Price – Director

Recently, the Chief Executive Officer has announced that he will be leaving RTTC, with his planned exit date early next month. RTTC has been searching for a replacement and has found a suitable candidate, Lynn Watson, who currently works for a local competitor. Lynn comes to RTTC with a very strong technical background and with a personal recommendation from Sarah Tov Ly. Lynn is very keen to join RTTC, but has stated she will only leave her current job if the "price is right." The Vice-President of Human Resources, Inge Axsater, was responsible for the negotiation of the salary. Once the salary was negotiated, Inge brought it forward to the compensation committee for approval. The salary and benefit package was four times the amount that the existing CEO was being paid. The compensation committee approved the salary and provided Lynn with an offer that she immediately accepted. The moment the shareholders became aware of the salary, they accused the board of incompetence, saying that such a large package should never have been approved.

The chair has asked you to review the process by which Lynn's salary was determined and identify any weaknesses in the process. He has also asked you to provide recommendations to rectify any weaknesses that you identify.

Required

Write a report to the chair, addressing his concerns.

Chapter 2: Cost Classifications

2.1 Sticks versus Bars

Jeff Ritchie and Ryan Collins have just finished fourth-year university and are passionate about starting their own business. Jeff has a bachelor of commerce degree and specialized in marketing. Ryan also has a bachelor of commerce and specialized in accounting. After a significant amount of research, they have two potential ideas. Their first idea is to manufacture hockey sticks and their second idea is to make a gluten-free energy bar. They have already rented a manufacturing facility; 80% of the space will be used for manufacturing the product and 20% will be for administration.

In order to get enough funding to start up their business, Jeff and Ryan have booked a preliminary meeting with the bank to determine if either of the ideas would allow their company to be eligible for a bank loan. The bank has asked them to prepare a schedule of the estimated costs associated with each of the ideas and to classify each cost as either a product cost or a period cost, and as either a fixed cost or a variable cost. The bank tends to favour ventures that have a low amount of fixed period costs relative to sales earned. Ryan and Jeff had prepared a pro forma income statement (Exhibit 1) for each option, but did not think to classify the costs in the manner that the bank had requested. As Ryan has a strong accounting background, he offered to prepare a memo to the bank with the cost classifications it is asking for. Jeff also asked him to determine which venture he believes the bank will favour.

Required

Assume the role of Ryan and write a letter to the bank addressing its request. Also write a letter to Jeff describing which manufacturing venture would likely be favoured by the bank.

EXHIBIT 1 – PRO FORMA FINANCIAL STATEMENTS
Annual Pro Forma Income Statement
Hockey Sticks
*Assumes 60,000 hockey sticks are sold per year

Sales	$ 6,420,000
Fibreglass	1,200,000
Graphite	1,080,000
Kevlar	642,000
Depreciation—Vehicles	7,500
Depreciation—Equipment	28,000
Depreciation—Office furniture	3,000
Depreciation—Computers	2,500
Distribution expenses	260,000
Janitorial expenses	80,000
Wages—Ryan (administrative)	42,000
Wages—Jeff (administrative)	42,000
Wages—Assembly workers	900,000
Wages—Quality assurance staff	510,000
Marketing expenses	55,000
Rent	60,000
Income	**$1,508,000**

Annual Pro Forma Income Statement
Gluten-Free Energy Bars
*Assumes 850,000 gluten-free energy bars are sold per year

Sales	$2,541,500
Ingredients	416,500
Packaging	102,000
Food inspection costs	187,000
Depreciation—Equipment	30,000
Depreciation—Vehicles	7,500
Depreciation—Office equipment	4,000
Depreciation—Computers	1,400
Janitorial expenses	10,000
Wages—Ryan (administrative)	42,000
Wages—Jeff (administrative)	42,000
Wages—Quality assurance	765,000
Marketing expenses	55,000
Rent	60,000
Income	**$ 819,100**

2.2 McDoodles

Contributed by
Patricia Stringer CA, CMA
Instructor, University of Alberta, Edmonton

McDoodles is a quick-service restaurant with a global presence. McDoodles sells a signature hamburger, the "Mammoth," along with sweet potato french fries with an aioli sauce, and fountain pop. Changes in the industry have caused McDoodles to review the preparation and delivery of its food products.

Recently McDoodles' research and development team has developed and patented a process to flash "suspend" its fully cooked products. The process involves cooking the products (hamburgers and french fries) and dressing them with their required garnishes: lettuce, tomato, pickle, onion, and special sauce for the Mammoth and salt and aioli sauce for the french fries. Once the products are at the correct serving temperature and presentation, the products are individually put into the "preserver" machine, where the item is suspended at its serving temperature and sealed into a special reusable container.

The suspension of the Mammoth and french fries puts the products into a state that can only be reversed using the "refresher" machine, which looks like an overly large microwave. The products can be kept in the suspended state for an extended period of time. (To date, McDoodles has tested products suspended for more than one year with perfect results.)

The product is then shipped to the individual McDoodles' locations where the product can be "unsuspended" as needed. The process to unsuspend is to put the product or multiple products (in their individual containers) into the refresher for one second. (Each location has been equipped with a refresher.) The product is then back at its perfect selling temperature and quality.

As some customers prefer not to have some garnishes on their Mammoth, individual garnishes and plain Mammoths can also be flash suspended. Studies have shown that 90% of McDoodles customers purchase their Mammoths with all garnishes and only 10% have at least one garnish omitted.

The use of the refresher at the restaurant eliminates the need for a kitchen. This also means that kitchen staff will no longer be required. Each location may need an employee to work the refresher and/or dress the plain Mammoths with the individual garnishes.

You are the cost accountant for McDoodles. The new flash suspension system to process the Mammoth and french fries starts next week.

As part of your job, you are required to analyze cost information for McDoodles. You have collected the main existing categories used for costs at McDoodles. The cost categories, in alphabetical order, are in Exhibit 1.

Required

    (a) Classify the cost categories as product or period costs.

    (b) For the cost categories you have noted as product costs in part (a), indicate whether the cost is a direct material, direct labour, or manufacturing overhead.

EXHIBIT 1 – MCDOODLES' COST CATEGORIES

1. Accounting department salaries
2. Aioli sauce for french fries (5-kg container)
3. Amortization of the fryer (for deep-frying french fries)
4. Amortization of the grill (for making Mammoths)
5. Amortization of the preserver
6. Amortization of the refresher
7. Amortization of restaurant tables and chairs
8. Cash register lease
9. Cash register supplies
10. Cups, lids, and straws for pop (individual sleeves of 100 each)
11. Factory cleaning supplies
12. Factory cooking supplies
13. Factory equipment maintenance costs
14. Fountain pop syrup
15. Fountain pop system rent
16. Heat, light, and power for the factory
17. Heat, light, and power for the restaurant
18. Insurance for the factory
19. Insurance for the restaurant
20. Lettuce (box of 5 heads of lettuce)
21. Mammoth buns (bag of 20 buns)
22. Mammoth patties used (box of 20 frozen patties)
23. Oil for cooking french fries (6-kg tub)
24. Onions (approximately 10 in a box)
25. Pickles (5-kg jar)
26. Packaging supplies (to package Mammoths and french fries at restaurant)
27. Preserver supplies (to package Mammoths and french fries)
28. President's salary
29. Restaurant cleaning supplies
30. Restaurant rent
31. Salaries and benefits of factory supervisors
32. Salary of restaurant manager
33. Salt (10-kg box)
34. Security guard for the factory
35. Special sauce for Mammoth (20-kg tub)
36. Sweet potatoes (20-kg bag)
37. Tomatoes (approximately 10 in a box)
38. Wages and benefits for Mammoth cooks
39. Wages and benefits for preserver staff
40. Wages and benefits for restaurant cashier/assembler

2.3 Johnny's Lawn Service

Contributed by
Sandy Qu PhD, CGA
Associate Professor, Schulich School of Business, York University, Toronto

---

Johnny Wong, a third-year university student majoring in international business, started his own part-time business in May 20X3, providing a grass-cutting service in the neighbourhood where he lives with his parents.

Before starting this, Johnny had been helping out an elderly neighbour, Jabir, who had broken his leg in an accident. Initially Jabir would treat Johnny to lunch and afternoon tea as a thank-you. After a couple of times, Jabir insisted on paying Johnny for the grass-cutting. It was also Jabir who suggested Johnny consider starting a business to help the neighbourhood seniors and those who might be too busy to cut their own lawns. Johnny gave this some serious thought before deciding to go ahead. The neighbourhood has hundreds of large homes with big lawns, so it would provide enough business opportunity. He also thought it would be a great form of outdoor exercise during the summer as well as a decent way to make some money to pay for tuition and help out people. A lawn business would be a different experience since Johnny has usually spent his summer (from May to August) working full-time (five days a week) in McDonald's for $10 an hour.

Johnny paid $200 for expenses related to business registration, which is valid for five years. He purchased a used high-power gas lawn mower plus some cleaning tools at a garage sale for $250 and he was told the lawn mower would last for at least five summers. He borrowed the money interest-free from his parents and promised he would pay it back by the end of the summer. He charges customers $25 each visit, cutting both the front and back yard, and it typically takes him about an hour and a half to finish the job, plus another 15 to 20 minutes or so to clean up the clippings and the mower itself. To advertise the business, Johnny posted flyers on central mailbox stations and sometimes knocked on doors and left a flyer if no one was at home. In total, the flyers and printing cost about $300.

In order to attract more regular customers during the summer months in which Johnny was able to work full-time, he offered a discounted price of $80 per month (that is, $20 per visit) if the customer signs up for a weekly service for the entire summer (from June to August). This promotion worked very well, since by the end of May he had more than 30 customers signed up for the monthly discount. Johnny kept a detailed journal of all his customers, recording their addresses, telephone numbers, the date and time of service, and the payment they have made.

The summer of 20X3 had a lot of rain and the grass grew fast. Johnny was kept busy all summer long and occasionally he would hire his brother Luke to help out. Luke just finished his last year in high school and Johnny agreed to pay him $10 for every job he did. The total would be paid by the end of the summer. On average, Johnny worked five days a week, with four to six customer visits per day. Most of his time was spent cutting the lawn, with 20% of his time spent managing customer- and payment-related information. For most customers, Johnny would need to drive a short distance (usually less than 10 minutes) in his car carrying his lawn mower. This cost him extra gasoline and time. Johnny kept all the receipts for amounts he spent buying gas for the lawn mower as well as for his car. Since gas prices have been at an all-time high, Johnny felt fortunate that he did not have to drive too far to provide services. By the end of August, Johnny still had about $150 worth of gas left for the lawn mower.

By the end of September, Johnny thought it was time to prepare an income statement for the period from May to August to see how well his business had been running (Exhibit 1). Not shown on the income statement is the fact that he needs to pay back the money he borrowed from his parents.

When Johnny started his business, he thought that it would be more profitable than working in McDonald's but he was disappointed to see on the income statement that he was wrong. He was therefore considering whether it was worthwhile to continue the business next summer, despite the fact that quite a number of satisfied neighbours were keen to sign up next year. One factor for Johnny to consider in his decision is that if the business is to be discontinued, the money he spent on the registration, insurance, and equipment would be totally wasted.

Required

Help Johnny evaluate the business by identifying and classifying his costs. Is this more profitable than working at McDonald's? Is there any opportunity cost for running the business for Johnny?

EXHIBIT 1 – INCOME STATEMENT
JOHNNY'S LAWN SERVICE
Income Statement
For the Period Ended August 31, 20X3

Revenues		$10,100
Gas for lawn mower	$1,060	
Gas for Johnny's car	800	
Lawn mower, cleaning tools, and other equipment	250	
Business registration	200	
Insurance	330	
Advertising	300	
Luke's wages	1,000	
Johnny's wages	6,400	
Total expenses		10,340
Operating income		$ (240)

3.1 Just the Right Stuff

April 7, 20X3

You have just finished your third year of university and are looking for a summer job. You are registered in an accounting program, and hope to one day earn a professional accounting designation. As you are job searching, you come across a unique posting:

WANTED: ACCOUNTING SUMMER STUDENT

THE DEETS: Want to work at a cool place and be an accountant at the same time?? We have JUST the place for you! We are a group of students starting our own business. We don't have much money, but there should be enough to pay you enough to party and eat for four months. One day, we all could be rich. As we are a start-up, we can't give you too much of the scoop. E-mail us your resumé and we might e-mail you for an interview.

E-mail: justtherightstuff@justtherightstuff.com

April 20, 20X3

After meeting with Ajay and Mona, the two co-founders of Just the Right Stuff, you accept the position willingly. You are excited to help them get their new business off the ground and can't wait to see the opportunities it will bring.

May 1, 20X3

On your first day of work, Ajay asks you to review their business proposal, which should give you an understanding of the business at Just the Right Stuff. From your reading, you understand the following:

Funding

Just the Right Stuff has just been awarded a grant from the government to use as start-up funds. Both Ajay and Mona have received money from family who love the idea and wanted to make an investment. The total amount of start-up funds is $50,000. Ajay and Mona hope to earn a 15% return on their investment.

The Idea

Just the Right Stuff is an on-line graphic design business. If a person needs a design, they can post their detailed request on-line and the price they are willing to pay for the design. Just the Right Stuff has three graphic designers. If there is a designer willing to accept the job, the job will proceed as long as the price suggested by the customer is reasonable. The customer will receive a soft copy of the design, as well as a professional printed design. Each design will be printed on high-quality paper. The number of pages used will depend on the size of the design.

Your Job

As the business gets off the ground, there will be many jobs for you, including budgeting, forecasting, purchasing, invoicing, and financial reporting. However, right now, Mona and Ajay need to understand the best way to determine whether or not they should accept a design.

After a discussion with them, you understand that in order to get the company going, they would accept virtually any job that doesn't result in a loss. They have provided you with a list of expenses (Exhibit 1) and asked you to develop a process that should be considered whenever a job design is posted to help determine whether they should accept the job. Ajay and Mona expect that they will have 5,000 designs posted to the website in the first year and intend to produce 3,000. On average, each design will be printed on two pages of paper.

Required

Provide Mona and Ajay with the details of your proposed process for them to consider whether to accept a design job.

EXHIBIT 1 – EXPECTED COSTS

Cost Item	Estimated Totals per Year	Selected Notes
Printer ink	$ 3,000	
Specialty paper	5,000	For 2,500 sheets
Graphic designers' wages	120,000	Graphic designers are paid $20 per hour
Co-founders' wages	20,000	$10,000 each
Accountant's wages	5,000	
Website	9,000	
Shipping	1,000	
Total	**$163,000**	

3.2 Silk Screen Inc.

Contributed by
Mary M. Oxner PhD, CA, CFA
Associate Professor, Gerald Schwartz School of Business, St. Francis Xavier University, Antigonish

---

Over the last three years, the owner of Silk Screen Inc., Scott White, has seen his business increase significantly. Scott decided to start a silk-screening business in the city of the university from which he graduated three years ago. Scott recognized that there was a market for silk-screened products, especially T-shirts. The various varsity teams, university clubs, minor hockey teams, soccer camps, festivals, and so on all require T-shirts with various designs and new T-shirts each year. All of these organizations previously had to order silk-screened products from a provider 100 km out of the city and had to build in enough lead time for ordering, which was often difficult because of the complexities in anticipating demand.

Scott developed his business model by charging a flat rate per T-shirt. The T-shirts are of good quality and Scott, who has design experience, can help the teams and organizations in designing their T-shirts. As the business grew, customers' design expectations also grew, becoming more elaborate and incorporating more colours. Scott is pleased with the growth of the business but is concerned about the profit margin, which appears to be shrinking. He would like to achieve an average profit margin of 25% on cost.

Scott shared with his accountant his suspicions that the elaborate designs, which require more time and ink in the silk-screening process, are hurting the bottom line. For example, the investment society of the local university has a simple design for its T-shirts, just a black dollar sign. The local dance group, however, requires T-shirts with an elaborate design—multiple dancers, costumes, and shoe types—using six colours. The only difference in the sales price of the T-shirts is the type of shirt that the customer requests. Currently, 50/50 (50% cotton, 50% polyester) T-shirts, 100% cotton T-shirts, and 100% cotton golf shirts each cost wholesale $10, $15, and $25, respectively. Scott sells these T-shirts to customers for $20, $25, and $40, respectively, regardless of the design and the number of colours of ink. Elaborate designs and numerous ink colours require more set-up time, more ink, and more colours.

Silk-screen printing is a technique in which a stencil is used to apply an image to an object, such as a T-shirt. The stencil forms open areas through which ink is transferred. The ink is transferred onto the object by moving a blade or squeegee across the stencil and pushing the ink through the stencil onto the object. Only one colour can be applied at any one time and each colour requires its own stencil. More elaborate designs require more complex stencils and colours. Because only one colour can be applied at any one time, designs with multiple colours require an application for each colour and a stencil for each colour. Consequently, the costs for silk screening relate to the time to develop the design, the cost of each colour of ink, and the time to apply each colour.

Scott's accountant suggested that they review the cost of different designs and colours of representative T-shirt orders that he has manufactured in the recent month. Although Scott's current pricing approach is to charge a single price for every design, he is now interested in looking at costing, pricing, and profit analysis using a new approach that accumulates costs by order; that is, a job-order costing system. The job-order costing system that Scott envisions allocates costs to orders based on the type of T-shirt, the number of colours of ink used in the design, and the cost of the ink colours used. The number of colours depends on the complexity of the design and each colour of ink is priced separately. (See Exhibit 1 for a listing of common colours of ink and their costs.)

Scott has pulled two representative customer orders for comparison (both used 100% cotton T-shirts): Customer #1 (the Autism Awareness Society) used five colours (black, yellow, red, orange, and fuchsia) and Customer #2 (a minor hockey under-12 team) used two colours (black and white only). Orders are typically placed in quantities of 100 T-shirts. Scott plans to continue to allocate overhead costs using a predetermined rate of $2.50 per T-shirt; those overhead costs include rent, equipment maintenance and depreciation, utilities, part-time staff and owner salaries, and office supplies.

Required

Prepare a report for Scott White that addresses the following:

(a) Calculate the cost of the two representative customer orders using the proposed job-order costing system envisioned by Scott. Calculate the profit margin of each T-shirt in the two representative customer orders using the current pricing scheme (that is, single price).

(b) Using the cost from the proposed job-order costing system as the basis for determining price, determine the appropriate price to charge for each T-shirt for the two representative customer orders.

(c) Scott designs and prepares the stencils on the computer. He doesn't feel that he needs to include his design time and the cost of printing the stencils in the direct cost of the T-shirts because the computer generates both the designs and the stencil printing. Advise Scott as to whether he should incorporate the design and stencil-printing costs into his retail prices.

(d) What factors should Scott consider if he refines the proposed job-order costing approach to his costing and pricing scheme?

EXHIBIT 1 – COST PER COLOUR APPLICATION

Colour	Cost per 100 ml of ink	Average Cost per Application per T-Shirt
White	$ 5.00	$1.00
Black	$ 5.00	$1.00
Red	$10.00	$2.00
Blue	$12.00	$2.25
Yellow	$12.00	$2.25
Purple	$14.00	$2.25
Orange	$15.00	$3.00
Fuchsia	$20.00	$4.00

3.3 Supermix Corp.

Contributed by
Sandy Qu PhD, CGA
Associate Professor, Schulich School of Business, York University, Toronto

Supermix Corporation is a world leader in designing and manufacturing high-end blending equipment. Its customers expect first-class blending performance with commercial quality and unsurpassed engineering. It builds and markets two lines of quality kitchen blenders: the Ultimate, for commercial use by professional chefs in the food service and hospitality industries, and the Superior, for consumer use by health-conscious home cooks who care about preparing fresh, flavourful food and beverages from whole-food ingredients. Supermix employs more than 300 people, has a global market in more than 60 countries, and continues to be recognized as a leader in product innovation.

The production process is heavily automated, relying on advanced blending and blades technologies. Manufacturing overhead is applied on the basis of machine hours using a plant-wide predetermined overhead rate. This single rate works well for both the Ultimate and the Superior lines since the Ultimate blenders will use more machine hours compared with the Superior line in order to configure sharper and faster blades for commercial use. The accuracy of the overhead rate is important because it is used throughout the year and is a key factor in determining the product price.

Jason Smith, CEO of Supermix, and Lucy Katanski, the CFO, are facing some tough decisions lately. A top management team meeting was held a couple of days ago and a new proposal was under heated discussion. George Takeuchi, the production manager for the commercial line, has proposed purchasing an Automated Blade Designing System (ABDS), which configures a more competitive blender model, the Q series, for heavier-duty commercial use. Utilizing the ABDS technology, the Q series blender is an all-in-one system that can make up to 150 drinks per hour, and minimizes ingredient waste, which will help commercial clients achieve cost efficiency and maximize profits. George was very enthusiastic and believed that the new system would allow Supermix to produce the best commercial grade blender available on the market that no competitors can beat. In addition, George suggested that this new technology would reduce the total machine hours spent on producing the Ultimate products by one third. Since the current production is at full capacity, this will ease constraint, because some machines are aging. If there is extra capacity, it may even allow Supermix to produce more or better blenders in the consumer Superior line.

Ben Sowlati, the production manager for the consumer line, has some concerns about how the ABDS would affect the current overhead rate. Currently, a preliminary estimate for the next fiscal year is based on an estimated total manufacturing overhead cost of $9,180,000 and an estimated 153,000 total machine hours, with two thirds spent producing the Ultimate and one third on the Superior. With the new ABDS system, apparently the overhead will have to be recalculated, factoring in the purchase price of the system, which is $899,000, and an installation cost of $50,000. Moreover, Ben is still a bit concerned about the effect of introducing the new system on his department. Even though there might be more machine hours available for the consumer products, according to what George has suggested, Ben is not sure whether this will have an adverse impact on the Superior line since the ABDS system is focused on improving commercial production. Since the cost of the new system is substantial, Ben would like Jason and Lucy to consider the use of a separate overhead rate for each department.

Required

Evaluate the effect of the proposal to introduce the ABDS system on overhead allocation and provide a recommendation to Jason Smith and Lucy Katanski. Assume that Supermix uses straight-line depreciation and the new system is expected to last for five years with no residual value.

4.1 Fantastic Plastic Inc.

This case involves you doing an activity with Lego blocks. Your instructor will either give you Lego blocks to work with in a group, or will demonstrate this at the front of the room with a small group of students.

You work in the accounting department of Fantastic Plastic Inc., a factory that makes plastic items. Fantastic Plastic's assembly department makes one product and all units of the product are identical. Once units are completed in the assembly department, they go to the packaging department. A new staff accountant, Nithya, has joined the team but she has no experience in a factory and doesn't fully understand process costing. To help her, you use Lego to demonstrate the principles of process costing.

Part A – Equivalent Units

First, you show Nithya how to convert physical units into equivalent units. To demonstrate this, your first task is to design a sample product with the Lego blocks. Your product can be as simple or as complex as you want, depending on the different types of blocks you have, as long as each unit of your product is identical.

For simplicity, your instructor may ask you to assume there are no units in beginning inventory. Your instructor will tell you when to start making your product and will give you a specified amount of time for production (for example, 5 minutes). For our purposes, this time represents one month in Fantastic Plastic. Let's call it our 5-minute month.

During these 5 minutes, make as many units of your product as you can. When you start to make a unit, take out enough blocks to make that unit (for example, one red block, one blue block, and two yellow blocks), finish making it, and then start another unit. Or you can make two units at a time, depending on how complex your product is. This represents the continuous production process typical in process costing. Keep all the units you have finished in one area of your desk as this represents your units completed. At the end of the 5 minutes, stop making your product and leave any units that you are still working on as this represents your units in ending work-in-process.

Required

Complete the following to show Nithya how to calculate the number of equivalent units completed and transferred to the packaging department and the number of equivalent units in ending work-in-process in the assembly department.

(a) Calculate the following:

1. number of physical units completed and transferred to the packaging department

2. number of physical units in ending work-in-process in the assembly department

(b) Because each unit is identical, convert physical units into equivalent whole units. For example, if your finished product has 10 different blocks and your units in work-in-process have half of these blocks in place, then your ending work-in-process is 50% complete with respect to direct materials.

(c) Estimate equivalent units in terms of conversion costs (direct labour and overhead). If you assume that conversion costs are applied to the product equally throughout the production process, then if the units are, say, 80% of the way through the production process in the assembly department, they will have 80% of the conversion costs.

(d) With this information, you can now calculate the following:

1. number of equivalent units (for direct materials and conversion costs) completed and transferred to the packaging department (this will be the same as your physical units because they are finished)

2. number of equivalent units (for direct materials and conversion costs) in ending work-in-process in the assembly department

You should now know the total physical units for the 5-minute month as well as the number of equivalent units this represents.

Part B – Costs

Now you need to show Nithya how to calculate the costs of your units completed and transferred out as well as the cost of your units in ending work-in-process.

Required

(a) Make a list of the different types of costs that will be incurred in this assembly department; for example, the cost of materials and labour as well as any overhead costs you think should be included. Your classroom is your pretend factory, so look around the room to get an idea of the different costs that would be included in overhead.

(b) Once you have a list of your types of costs, you need to assign a dollar amount to them. Your instructor will either give you these costs (for example, red blocks cost $0.10 each, blue blocks cost $0.15) or will ask you to estimate them. Remember that labour and overhead are combined into one category called conversion costs, so you will end up with totals for two categories: direct materials and conversion costs.

(c) When you have your cost of direct materials and conversion costs, calculate a cost per equivalent unit for direct materials and conversion costs.

(d) Finally, apply these unit costs to the units completed and transferred out and to the units in ending work-in-process at the end of your 5-minute month.

4.2 Fudge Delights Inc.

Contributed by
Mary M. Oxner PhD, CA, CFA
Associate Professor, Gerald Schwartz School of Business, St. Francis Xavier University, Antigonish

Sarah Cameron has loved confections her whole life and as a young girl learned how to make peanut brittle, fudge, and toffee from her grandmother. Sarah has continued the candy-making tradition in her family throughout her life and made fudge at Christmas and other holidays for friends and family and also sold fudge at craft shows and bazaars. Several years ago, Sarah explored the idea of making and selling her own brand of confections on a commercial basis. When the opportunity arose and her business plan allowed, Sarah opened a candy store, Fudge Delights Inc., in which she sells a variety of candies and confections, many of which remind customers of candy they had as kids. In addition to the candy that she buys from suppliers, Sarah makes different flavours of fudge for sale in her store. Because fudge has a reasonable shelf life, Sarah can make it in large batches weeks ahead of the time anticipated for sale. Sarah's favourite flavours include classic maple, chocolate chip chocolate, maple walnut, cherries and cream, chocolate mint julep, lemon drop, and toffee almond. From Sarah's perspective, the variety and number of flavours is as large as one's imagination. Sarah's confectionary store has earned a great reputation for premium confections and high-quality fudge, resulting in a 50% increase in sales year over year for the last four years.

There are many ways to make fudge. Sarah uses the same basic technique for all the varieties. To make the fudge, she cooks a sugar syrup to the soft-ball stage, lets it cool for a specified amount of time, and then agitates it until crystals form that are smaller than the original sugar crystals; the agitation is primarily what gives fudge its creamy texture. Sarah does not vary the approach to making fudge but does vary the ingredients to create the different flavours. Currently Sarah does not make custom flavours for customers but might consider doing so in the future if time and demand allow. The fudge is sold in ½-lb. and 1-lb. slabs at a price of $7.00 per ½ lb. or $12.00 for 1 lb. regardless of the flavour of fudge. (Homemade fudge is typically sold by the pound in Canada.)

In Sarah's previous job with a large international soap maker, she learned the need for refined cost information to make good decisions about pricing and profitability analyses of various product lines. Several years ago when Sarah set up her business, she adopted a job-order system for costing the various kinds of fudge. Sarah has been quite diligent about keeping very detailed records for each batch of fudge. Sarah processes all the fudge on-site in small batches by flavour. For each batch, Sarah collects information on the amount of butter, sugar, milk, and other ingredients like chocolate, walnuts, vanilla extract, hazelnuts, and peanut butter. The basic fudge recipe and process is exactly the same for the various flavours of fudge except at the end, when different ingredients are added. The information on each batch is eventually recorded and stored on an electronic index card. The information allows Sarah to best understand the difference in the cost of each batch of fudge. Although the cost information does not affect the selling price of the fudge (because the store policy is to price all fudge at the same price), it does allow Sarah to know which flavours are more costly. Ultimately, this information could result in a flavour being dropped from her product line or sold at a premium price.

With the growth in the business, Sarah has hired an additional fudge maker, Zhanna, and is training her in the art of making fudge that meets Sarah's standards. Zhanna, like Sarah, has made fudge for most of her life. However, unlike Sarah, Zhanna has no affinity for the costing system that Sarah has put in place. Zhanna is questioning whether it makes sense to record the details that Sarah requires. The manual entry of each ingredient added to the batch of fudge takes as much time as making the batch itself. Zhanna is questioning whether the information really is that useful given that the prices are the same and they mostly make batches of their most popular flavours. Sarah has decided to take a second glance at the information she has been collecting during the fudge-making process to ensure the cost data collected provide useful information about overall cost.

The ingredients for making one batch (10 lb.) of fudge for four of the most popular flavours of fudge are shown in Exhibit 1.

Sarah has set up a record-keeping system such that the amount used in each batch is recorded by hand as the ingredient is added. The recording is usually done by entering the ingredient amounts on a card and then using the card to enter the data into an electronic index card and ultimately an electronic spreadsheet. At the end of the month, Sarah reviews the data entry by batch and calculates the total cost of the batch. At the end of the year, Sarah reviews the batch data but does no analysis with the data; however, the possibility of analysis exists because the data are available.

The costs of the ingredients, on average, are in Exhibit 2.

Sarah would like to demonstrate that the cost data collected provide valuable insight into the costs of the various flavours of fudge and would like to be able to justify her use of job-order costing. Sarah knows that the alternative is to adopt a process costing system but is hesitant about changing costing approaches. She wants to have good cost data for decision-making and is hesitant to switch to process costing because she fears a loss of refined data from her costing system and the implications on cost of any changes in ingredients (such as the fluctuation in the price of white sugar last year).

Required

Prepare a report for Sarah Cameron that addresses the following:

(a) Calculate the cost per pound of each of the four most popular flavours of fudge produced by Fudge Delights. Also, calculate the profitability of each of those flavours of fudge.

(b) Calculate the differential cost per pound and differential profitability per pound between each costing method of those four flavours.

(c) Sarah's job-order costing system provides valuable cost and profitability information about the various batches of different flavours of fudge. Data like the cost information Sarah is collecting can be used to make decisions about production levels, pricing, and product offerings. Discuss how these data can be used to make decisions.

(d) Advise Sarah Cameron on whether she should continue with her current costing approach.

EXHIBIT 1 – INGREDIENTS FOR MAKING ONE BATCH OF THE FOUR MOST POPULAR FUDGE FLAVOURS

10-lb. Batches (c = cup)	Classic Maple Walnut	Classic Chocolate	Peanut Butter with Peanuts	Chocolate Turtle
Sugar	30 c	30 c	30 c	30 c
Butter	5 c	5 c	5 c	5 c
Maple syrup	¾ c	-	-	-
Chocolate syrup	-	2¼ c	-	⅘ c
Walnuts	1¼ c	-	-	-
Peanut butter	-	-	2½ c	
Peanuts	-	-	1¼ c	1¼ c
Caramel	-	-	-	1¼ c

EXHIBIT 2 – AVERAGE COST OF FUDGE INGREDIENTS

Ingredient	Lot Size	Cost per Lot Size
Sugar	100 cups	$20.00
Butter	10 cups	$20.00
Maple syrup	10 cups	$25.00
Chocolate syrup	15 cups	$23.00
Walnuts	20 cups	$25.00
Peanut butter	20 cups	$20.00
Peanuts	20 cups	$15.00
Caramel	25 cups	$25.00

Chapter 5: Activity-Based Costing

5.1 TeaTime.com

After 10 years of working as an internal auditor at a large insurance company, Patrick Vickers decided to realize his dream of running his own business. He had a young family and wanted the flexibility in hours that a small business would provide. His job at the insurance company gave him the chance to travel to Asia, where he developed a love of fine tea. After years of dreaming, planning, and saving, he started TeaTime.com in January 2012. While he expected business to be slow at first, he was disappointed in the financial results in his first year of operations. (See Exhibit 1.)

TeaTime.com is an on-line company that provides a premium tea delivery service to its members. For $20 per month, members receive a package containing four different blends of loose-leaf tea, which is carefully selected by Patrick through his contacts in Asia. Each month the blends of tea changes, allowing Patrick to fulfill his goals of bringing a variety of premium Asian tea to the Canadian market as well as supporting many of the small tea producers he got to know in his travels to Asia.

Patrick did his research before deciding to open TeaTime.com. Tea is one of the most popular drinks in the world and consumption of tea in Canada is increasing as consumers are becoming more aware of its health benefits. Patrick felt that busy Canadians would appreciate the convenience of having premium tea delivered to their door and that the $20 monthly fee would be enough to cover his costs plus give him some income to support his family.

The business model Patrick set up is simple. Members subscribe to the service on the TeaTime.com website. After completing a form with name, address, and credit card information, members start receiving their monthly boxes of tea. Recognizing that members may need to suspend deliveries for vacations or other reasons, the website has a spot where members can pause and restart their accounts at any time. Members can also access a discussion board where they can leave comments about their favourite blends of tea. The tea is pre-ordered from Asia and packaged in TeaTime.com's office space, which Patrick rents from his uncle at a reasonable rate.

Demand was strong enough in the first year that Patrick needed to hire four part-time staff to help him run the company. One staff member is responsible for the website and the member accounts. The other three package the tea and send it to members. Being close to a large university, Patrick easily filled the four part-time positions with students hoping to earn some extra money. Because of Patrick's experience in Asia, he has kept control of selecting and ordering the tea from the Asian suppliers. With his background in internal audit, Patrick keeps tight control of the company operations.

Despite all of Patrick's hard work, he is worried about whether his business will be able to generate enough profit to support his family. He knows that competition is tough, with premium tea shops in many convenient locations. If he could increase the number of members, he believes TeaTime.com could become profitable. He remembers learning about activity-based costing in university and wants to see if it could be used to help his company. He figured he would talk to his staff to see if they could provide any insight on the various activities of the business. (The information they provided is in Exhibit 2.) If TeaTime.com did not start to generate profits, he might have to go back to work at the insurance company. He was very well respected when he resigned, and his boss did say to contact him in the future if he ever needed work.

Required

1. Using a case format, prepare a report to Patrick highlighting the issues facing TeaTime.com.
2. Using the information from Exhibit 2, develop an Income Statement based on activity-based costing information.
3. Include recommendations as to what Patrick should do to turn a profit.

EXHIBIT 1 – TEATIME.COM FINANCIALS

TEATIME.COM
Income Statement
Year Ended December 31, 2012

Sales ($20/box × 324 boxes per month)	$ 77,760
Cost of goods sold ($8/box × 324 boxes per month)	31,104
Gross margin	46,656
Selling and administrative expenses	
Shipping	14,720
Marketing (website maintenance and advertising)	2,500
Rent	15,000
General and administrative	31,000
Total selling and administrative expenses	63,220
Operating income	($16,564)

Note: Cost of goods sold includes only the cost of the tea. All fixed overhead costs are included in selling and administrative expenses.

EXHIBIT 2 – INFORMATION FROM STAFF ABOUT THE OPERATIONS OF TEATIME.COM

After talking with his staff about TeaTime.com's selling and administrative expenses, Patrick decides to gather activity-based costing information for the shipping and general and administrative expenses and creates four activity cost pools. Shipping expenses are put in a "Package and ship tea" activity, and general and administrative expenses are split into three activities: "Set up member accounts," "Process pause and restart requests," and "Support members."

The following information was gathered from discussions with his staff about these activities for their first year of operations. Cost drivers were selected by Patrick and activity rates were determined through discussions with Patrick and his staff by estimating the percentage of time they spend on each activity.

Activity Cost Pool	Cost Driver	Total Quantity of Cost Driver	Activity Rate
Package and ship tea	Number of boxes shipped	3,888	$3.786 per box
Set up member accounts	Number of new members	150	$5 per member
Process pause and restart requests	Number of pause and restart requests	600	$49.584 per request
Support members	Number of members	150	$3.333 per member

5.2 ND University

Every year, the administration at ND University receives funding from the provincial government. This year, the government announced that due to budget cuts, it would be providing significantly less funding. Although ND University has yet to hear what the actual amount of the cut will be, the administration has decided to be proactive and try to identify ways to be more efficient with its money.

Each year, each department is given an equal amount of money per student registered in the department. For example, the accounting department is given the same amount per student as the science department. In addition, the university gives an equal amount per student regardless of whether the student is a graduate student or an undergraduate student. As such, the university assumes that all students cost the same amount of money. During a recent town hall meeting to discuss the budget cuts, one faculty member brought up the idea that some departments run cash surpluses at the end of each year, because they do not spend all the money provided per student. This might be an indication that some departments have students who cost the university less than others. One way to determine the cost of a student is by using the activity-based costing (ABC) method.

The president of the university, Mahmud Yazbek, has hired you, a young professional accountant, to help understand how activity-based costing may help to understand the cost of a student. President Yazbek has identified the major activities that the students engage in: lectures, labs, recruiting, administrative support, student life support, and educational student support. In addition, he has identified several overhead costs (Exhibit 1) and the percentage of time that each cost is spent on each activity. He has also provided you with a list of other information that he believes could act as cost drivers for each activity (Exhibit 2). Before President Yazbek rolls out this new method of costing, he would like to analyze whether the results will be different from the existing method. The traditional method of allocating these costs has been to add up all of the costs and divide the amount by the total number of students attending the university to determine the cost per student. He has asked you, first, to determine an appropriate cost driver and, second, to determine the cost of an accounting student (graduate and undergraduate) versus the cost of a science student (graduate and undergraduate). He would like you to prepare a report that includes your results and an analysis of your results.

Required

Prepare the report for President Yazbek.

EXHIBIT 1 – OVERHEAD COSTS

		Activity					
		Lectures	Labs	Recruiting	Administrative Support	Student Life Support	Educational Student Support
Professors' salaries	$21,851,700	65%	15%	5%	0%	5%	10%
Teaching assistants' salaries	3,015,000	5%	60%	0%	0%	10%	25%
Invigilators' salaries	753,750	0%	10%	0%	0%	0%	90%
Lab supervisors' salaries	1,130,625	0%	100%	0%	0%	0%	0%
Counsellors' salaries	1,350,000	0%	0%	10%	15%	65%	10%
Admission office salaries	1,200,000	0%	0%	80%	10%	10%	0%
Registrar's office salaries	480,000	0%	0%	25%	70%	5%	0%
Librarians' salaries	1,125,000	10%	15%	10%	5%	5%	55%
Food and hospitality salaries	10,500,000	5%	0%	0%	0%	95%	0%
Janitorial salaries	15,750,000	10%	10%	10%	5%	65%	0%

EXHIBIT 2 – COST DRIVER INFORMATION

Item	Total University	Accounting (Undergrad)	Accounting (Grad)	Science (Undergrad)	Science (Grad)
Number of students	14,645	650	60	5,000	150
Number of offers sent to potential students	4,760	179	18	1,875	64
Lecture hours	3,816,000	234,000	11,520	2,100,000	57,600
Lab hours	2,400,000	15,600	-	1,200,000	72,000

5.3 Soap Makers International

Contributed by
Mary M. Oxner PhD, CA, CFA
Associate Professor, Gerald Schwartz School of Business, St. Francis Xavier University, Antigonish

Several years ago, Ingrid Krause wanted some international experience and applied for a transfer to her company's soap division, which is located south of Warsaw, Poland. The soap division manufactures hand soap for use in a large number of settings, from hospitals to luxury hotels. Ingrid was awarded the transfer to the soap division and was assigned to the accounting department. She is responsible for overseeing the costing and profitability analysis of the various soaps and soap-making processes. During her tenure in the soap division, there were numerous changes in the number of soaps manufactured and the processes to make the different soaps. Consequently, Ingrid's position required her to consider changes in the accounting system to reflect the changes in the soap division's business.

For several decades, the company's soap-making process required a large labour force that manufactured and packaged the soap mostly by hand. Local economic changes meant that the labour force that the factory required was not as available as it had been in the past. As a result, the division was experiencing significant employee turnover, which often resulted in increased expenses related to training new hires, slower processing time, and more soap being rejected during inspections because of quality concerns. To address the issues related to the lack of labour availability, the division's management decided three years ago that automation was the way to go. Consequently, over the last three years, the soap-making processes have changed with the implementation of automation.

The automation of the soap-making process has allowed for a much larger variety of soap and packaging, a reduced direct labour force and direct labour costs, and a higher level of traceability of costs to the various soaps because of technological improvements. Soaps made for industrial applications require different ingredients, less time in processing, less time in finishing, and less time in and cheaper packaging than do soaps made for the hotel industry. The costs of materials and packaging are directly traceable to the various types of soaps through new software that uses bar codes and counters to trace direct material costs to the various soaps directly.

Ingrid feels that the current costing system should be revisited. The cost driver for allocation of the overhead costs (such as supervisory salaries and plant utilities) has always been direct labour cost. However, given the decline in the use of labour due to automation, Ingrid is questioning its suitability as a basis of allocation. Ingrid would like to explore activity-based costing to allocate overhead costs.

Ingrid has gathered cost data for two representative soaps: one sold to hospitals and one sold to hotels. Further, Ingrid has gathered data from the automated system on the amount of time each type of soap spends in the three manufacturing processes: processing, finishing, and packaging. The soap is produced in large batches; consequently, the data are adjusted to reflect the average cost per 100 g of soap. The data by type of soap for one month's production are in Exhibit 1.

Required

Prepare a report for Ingrid Krause that addresses her interest in exploring an activity-based costing (ABC) system while including the following:

(a) Is Ingrid's exploration of changing her cost allocation of overhead from a traditional approach (one cost driver for allocation) to an ABC approach (multiple cost drivers applied to multiple cost pools) justifiable? If so, explain to her why it is.

(b) Calculate the costs (of direct material, direct labour, and overhead) for each of the two representative types of soap using direct labour cost as the base for the allocation of overhead.

(c) Calculate the costs (of direct material, direct labour, and overhead) for each of the two representative types of soap using an ABC approach for the allocation of manufacturing costs.

(d) Do the cost allocation calculations provide support for an ABC approach? Explain.

(e) Would you advise Ingrid Krause to continue with her traditional costing approach or change to an ABC approach? Explain.

EXHIBIT 1 – COSTS FOR ONE MONTH'S PRODUCTION OF SOAP

Cost Components	Total	Costs per 100 g Soap	
		Industrial Soap (Hospital)	Luxury Soap (Hotel)
Direct materials	$4,000,000	$0.40	$0.80
Packaging	$2,000,000	$0.10	$0.60
Direct labour	$ 750,000	$0.14	$0.15
Manufacturing	$5,000,000	-	-
Processing	$2,500,000	-	-
Finishing	$1,500,000	-	-
Packaging	$1,000,000	-	-

EXHIBIT 2 – TIME REQUIRED FOR ONE MONTH'S PRODUCTION OF SOAP

Time Components	Total	Time per 100 g Soap	
		Industrial Soap (Hospital)	Luxury Soap (Hotel)
Processing	750,000 seconds	0.2 second	0.4 second
Finishing	300,000 seconds	0.03 second	0.4 second
Packaging	100,000 seconds	0.006 second	0.5 second

Chapter 6: Techniques for Measuring Fixed and Variable Costs

6.1 Trilogy Inc.

On December 15, 20X2, you began as the new CFO of Trilogy Inc. Trilogy produces and manufactures stainless steel water bottles. You inherited the business (along with all of its problems) from your father. Although your father is still alive and well, he has clearly stated he no longer wants anything to do with the business. It is now February 15, 20X3, and you have just finished preparing the 20X2 annual reports. During the process, you noticed many things that were unorganized and did not make sense. Also, you were very disappointed to learn that the company finished the year in a deficit. You believe Trilogy is a good company; however, there are many improvements that could be made to increase efficiency and boost profit. You just have to find them.

As a starting point, you called a meeting with the junior accountant. You asked him to provide you with a break-even analysis for Trilogy. The junior accountant stated that an analysis of this nature had never been performed and, although he could remember learning about a break-even analysis in university, he wasn't sure how to carry out this task. You realized that you should probably just do this on your own, as the junior accountant wasn't going to be much help. The junior accountant provided you with a list of revenues and expenses (Exhibit 1). He stated that most of the expenses are straightforward as to whether they are a fixed or a variable cost with the exception of the "other costs." After some discussion, you learn that the "other costs" are made up of depreciation, which is calculated using the straight-line method, and maintenance, which varies directly with the level of sales.

You quickly jot down a "to-do list" of the tasks you would like to complete by the end of the week:

1. Calculate the break-even point.
2. Use the break-even analysis to identify areas that could be improved to increase overall profitability.

Required

Complete both items on your to-do list. For item 2, discuss each of the areas you identify for improvement and outline the steps that would need to be taken in order to implement and achieve the improvement.

EXHIBIT 1 – TRILOGY INC.'S REVENUES AND EXPENSES

	Jan.	Feb.	March	April	May	June	July	Aug.	Sept.	Oct.	Nov.	Dec.	Total
Water bottles sold	311,567	456,756	564,042	567,000	663,099	654,000	657,900	675,000	780,000	576,990	678,965	768,990	7,354,309
Sales	$1,866,286	$2,735,968	$3,378,612	$3,396,330	$3,971,963	$3,917,460	$3,940,821	$4,043,250	$4,672,200	$3,456,170	$4,067,000	$4,606,250	$44,052,311
Steel	775,802	1,137,322	1,404,465	1,411,830	1,651,117	1,628,460	1,638,171	1,680,750	1,942,200	1,436,705	1,690,623	1,914,785	18,312,229
Plastic	124,627	182,702	225,617	226,800	265,240	261,600	263,160	270,000	312,000	230,796	271,586	307,596	2,941,724
Other material	62,313	91,351	112,808	113,400	132,620	130,800	131,580	135,000	156,000	115,398	135,793	153,798	1,470,862
Assembly wages	622,822	913,055	1,127,520	1,133,433	1,325,535	1,307,346	1,315,142	1,349,325	1,559,220	1,153,403	1,357,251	1,537,211	14,701,264
Administrative wages	400,000	400,000	400,000	400,000	400,000	400,000	400,000	400,000	400,000	400,000	400,000	400,000	4,800,000
Rent	105,000	105,000	105,000	105,000	105,000	105,000	105,000	105,000	105,000	105,000	105,000	105,000	1,260,000
Insurance	64,000	64,000	64,000	64,000	64,000	64,000	64,000	64,000	64,000	64,000	64,000	64,000	768,000
Other costs	108,545	131,351	166,345	153,400	187,208	170,800	197,896	195,250	227,200	161,168	190,730	210,716	2,100,609
Net income (loss)	$(396,823)	$(288,813)	$(227,143)	$(211,533)	$(158,757)	$(150,546)	$(174,128)	$(156,075)	$(93,420)	$(210,300)	$(147,983)	$(86,856)	$(2,302,377)

6.2 Au Naturel Incorporated

Contributed by
Sandy Kizan
Adjunct and Emeritus Professor, Athabasca University, Athabasca

Au Naturel Incorporated is feeling growing pains. After a successful first two years of operations, Au Naturel management is, for the first time, concerned about the potential of their business. The company began operations in 20X2 when the owner and founder, Jason Petrov, decided to enter the organic foods market. In early 20X1, after watching a documentary on food additives, Jason began purchasing organic foods for his family. Over the years, he noticed substantial growth in the organic section at the grocery store. Considering this opportunity, Jason thought he could use his background in food preparation and production to start his own organic foods company. Jason decided to open his business with a product that wasn't well represented on store shelves: organic peanut butter. He developed an organic peanut butter to be marketed under the Au Naturel brand and started manufacturing in February 20X2.

In the beginning, manufacturing peanut butter at the Au Naturel factory was a highly labour-intensive process. The factory used an assembly-line production model and each jar of peanut butter was handcrafted by six factory employees. By 20X3, Au Naturel was producing over 300 jars of peanut butter per day. Production schedules were based on demand volumes and employee hours varied from employee to employee each week. As a result, the company had high direct costs, which varied with the level of production. Direct costs included peanuts, packaging materials, manufacturing labour costs, and variable overhead costs. Indirect fixed costs were less substantial and mainly included production supervision, depreciation on equipment, warehouse rent, and property taxes.

With increasing demand levels (see Exhibit 1) and a capacity of only 100,000 jars of peanut butter per year using the existing process, Au Naturel management decided it was time to automate the factory.

At the beginning of 20X4, the company invested $2 million in new automation equipment that would be depreciated over a 10-year period. This enabled the plant to reduce its staffing from six to one factory worker and increase annual capacity to 180,000 jars of peanut butter. With the new automation process, one factory employee was retrained to be a plant supervisor with a salary of $63,000 per year. Although the product would no longer be handcrafted, the company believed that the high-quality ingredients and the company's attention to standards, cleanliness, and exceptional taste would maintain its image as a specialty food product. Jason was hoping, if this expansion was successful, to complete a further expansion in 20X6 of $2.5 million to increase plant capacity to 400,000 jars per year.

At the end of 20X4, however, Jason was shocked by the financial results of the automation implementation. Profits had fallen from the previous year even though sales increased by 20,000 units. Exhibit 2 provides a comparison of the incomes for 20X3 and 20X4.

Jason was worried! The automation of his factory seemed to have had a detrimental effect on profits. Jason calculated that, with total costs of $8.89 per unit ($4.15 + $3.96 + $0.20 + $0.58), he will only achieve a net income of $130,500 ($0.90 × 145,000 units) in 20X5 if Au Naturel meets the expected demand levels. This is less than what he was earning in 20X3 using the labour-intensive process. Jason is now wondering if automation was worth it. In the past, he could promote his peanut butter as a "handcrafted" product. Now he is wondering what advantage, if any, automation brings to his factory.

Jason has asked Anna Chui, an old friend and cost accountant, to help him assess further how the automation of the Au Naturel factory has impacted the company's bottom line.

Required

Assume the role of Anna and prepare a report for Jason looking at the following:

(a) Is Jason correct in stating that his income for 20X5 will be approximately $130,500? What flaws, if any, are there in Jason's assumptions regarding cost behaviour?

(b) If the revenues and cost rates remain at the same level as in 20X4, what should Au Naturel's net income be estimated at for 20X5? 20X6?

(c) Since the capacity of the new automated factory is only 180,000 jars of peanut butter (a level that will be reached in 20X6), should the company consider a further expansion of the plant? Assume the additional plant expansion cost will be depreciated over 10 years. For simplicity, assume all revenue and cost rates will remain the same as 20X4 levels and additional supervision of $68,000 would be required each year. What level of sales would be required to support this investment? If demand levels cap at 230,000 jars, would the further expansion be justified? Provide supporting calculations.

EXHIBIT 1 – DEMAND LEVELS FOR AU NATUREL ORGANIC PEANUT BUTTER

Year	Demand Level (Jars)
20X3	80,000 (actual demand)
20X4	100,000 (actual demand)
20X5	145,000 (expected)
20X6	180,000 (expected)

EXHIBIT 2 – COMPARATIVE INCOME STATEMENT

AU NATUREL PEANUT BUTTER
Income Statement

	20X3 Labour-Intensive Process		20X4 Automated Factory	
	Total	Per Unit	Total	Per Unit
Units sold	80,000		100,000	
Sales	$766,400.00	$9.58	$979,000.00	$9.79
Variable manufacturing costs:				
Direct materials (including peanuts, salt, and packaging materials)	278,320.04	$3.48	364,651.98	$3.65
Direct labour	96,860.16	$1.21	20,179.20	$0.20
Variable overhead	51,425.28	$0.64	29,721.60	$0.30
Total variable manufacturing costs	426,605.48	$5.33	414,552.78	$4.15
Fixed manufacturing overhead				
Rent	48,000.00	$0.60	52,500.00	$0.53
Production supervision	52,500.00	$0.66	127,800.00	$1.28
Property taxes	7,850.00	$0.10	7,850.00	$0.08
Depreciation	6,800.00	$0.09	206,800.00	$2.07
Total fixed manufacturing costs	115,150.00	$1.45	394,950.00	$3.96
Gross margin	224,644.52	$2.80	169,497.22	$1.68
Variable selling costs	16,000.00	$0.20	20,000.00	$0.20
General administrative costs	58,000.00	$0.73	58,000.00	$0.58
Net income before taxes	$150,644.52	$1.87	$ 91,497.22	$0.90

6.3 Omers Incorporated

Omers Incorporated is a car manufacturer that has been in business for over 60 years. The head office and manufacturing plant is located in Windsor, Ontario. The company currently manufactures a full lineup of vehicles, which includes three models of sedans, one sport utility vehicle, one minivan, and two pickup trucks. From time to time, the models are overhauled to have a new look; however, the lineup has stayed relatively stable over the last few years.

It is now October 4, 20X4, and you are an accountant working in the strategic planning department for the sedans. At the end of every third quarter, the company does a financial review on the sedans. Your boss, Nancy Huang, has asked you to help prepare for the review of the sedan models. A lot of information must be gathered before a thoughtful analysis can be produced. The information you provide will be just one part of a much larger analysis. She has provided you with limited information to get you started, found in Exhibit 1.

Required

Nancy Huang has asked you to prepare a detailed analysis considering each of the following items. With your report, provide a list of any limitations in your analysis.

(a) What is the contribution margin of each model? Under the current sales mix, how many of each model would be required to break even?

(b) What is the margin of safety and the degree of operating leverage for each model? Include an interpretation of your findings.

(c) How many more sedans would have to be sold to increase overall profit by 20% with a 40% tax rate?

EXHIBIT 1 – SEDAN COST INFORMATION TO DATE

Quarter 1			
Model name	Shadow	Moon	Ray	Total
Number of cars sold	162,500	192,500	300,000	655,000
Revenue	6,825,000,000	6,352,500,000	6,600,000,000	19,777,500,000
Direct materials	4,777,500,000	4,764,375,000	5,280,000,000	14,821,875,000
Labour	819,000,000	889,350,000	858,000,000	2,566,350,000
Maintenance	341,250,000	197,562,750	112,200,000	651,012,750
Administrative costs	273,000,000	508,200,000	594,000,000	1,375,200,000
Income (loss)	614,250,000	(6,987,750)	(244,200,000)	363,062,250

Quarter 2			
Model name	Shadow	Moon	Ray	Total
Number of cars sold	167,375	200,200	324,000	691,575
Revenue	7,029,750,000	6,606,600,000	7,128,000,000	20,764,350,000
Direct materials	4,780,230,000	4,822,818,000	5,559,840,000	15,162,888,000
Labour	913,867,500	924,924,000	869,616,000	2,708,407,500
Maintenance	421,785,000	264,264,000	71,280,000	757,329,000
Administrative costs	421,785,000	528,528,000	598,752,000	1,549,065,000
Income	492,082,500	66,066,000	28,512,000	586,660,500

Quarter 3			
Model name	Shadow	Moon	Ray	Total
Number of cars sold	184,113	218,218	353,160	755,491
Revenue	7,732,725,000	7,201,194,000	7,769,520,000	22,703,439,000
Direct materials	5,180,925,750	5,328,883,560	5,982,530,400	16,492,339,710
Labour	914,008,095	993,764,772	932,342,400	2,840,115,267
Maintenance	378,903,525	200,841,301	116,542,800	696,287,626
Administrative costs	471,696,225	648,107,460	606,022,560	1,725,826,245
Income	787,191,405	29,596,907	132,081,840	948,870,152

Total to Date			
Model name	Shadow	Moon	Ray	Total
Number of cars sold	513,988	610,918	977,160	2,102,066
Revenue	21,587,475,000	20,160,294,000	21,497,520,000	63,245,289,000
Direct materials	14,738,655,750	14,916,076,560	16,822,370,400	46,477,102,710
Labour	2,646,875,595	2,808,038,772	2,659,958,400	8,114,872,767
Maintenance	1,141,938,525	662,668,051	300,022,800	2,104,629,376
Administrative costs	1,166,481,225	1,684,835,460	1,798,774,560	4,650,091,245
Income (loss)	1,893,523,905	88,675,157	(83,606,160)	1,898,592,902

Notes:
1. Labour and maintenance are mixed costs (both fixed and variable costs).
2. Administrative costs are fixed costs.

Chapter 7: Cost-Volume-Profit

7.1 SUP Rides

Matthew, Thomas, and Michael Hahn are three brothers, all university students, who own SUP Rides, a small business that rents stand-up paddle (SUP) boards on the shores of Lake Huron in southern Ontario. Stand-up paddling is one of the fastest-growing water sports in the world. The sport began about 50 years ago when surfing instructors would stand on their boards to take pictures. Since then, the sport has taken off in popularity because it is relatively easy to learn, it provides physical benefits like improved strength and balance, and it provides mental benefits such as stress relief and relaxation.

Customers are typically teenagers looking to experience the laid-back SUP lifestyle. SUP Rides also promotes water safety to its customers and employees. Some things, like the weather, are out of their control, but the Hahn brothers believe that having a positive, fun attitude on the beach will help them attract customers. Currently they have not spent any money on advertising and they are the only company renting SUP boards in the area.

The brothers have been operating SUP Rides for the past two summers. The business operates for three months, from June 1 to August 31. They own four paddle boards, which they rent out for $25 per hour each. They estimate that on a monthly basis the boards are rented for a total of approximately 600 hours (4 boards × 30 days × 5 hours per day), bringing in monthly revenue of $15,000.

SUP Rides hires a summer student, Nadja, who is paid $15 per hour for the 600 hours the paddle boards are rented. Also, for each hour a paddle board is rented, the business incurs $3 in supplies costs to wax and prepare the boards.

SUP Rides incurs fixed costs for its three months of operations, including rent and salary. The business rents a beachside kiosk from the local municipality for three months for $1,500 per month and stores the boards and other equipment in the Hahn parents' basement for free the rest of the year. Michael is paid a salary of $1,000 per month for three months because he works full-time for the business in the summer. The other brothers, Matthew and Thomas, work full-time in the city and come up on weekends but are not involved in the business on a day-to-day basis. SUP Rides purchased four boards two years ago for $900 each. The boards are depreciated on a straight-line basis and are expected to last three years.

While the brothers enjoy owning SUP Rides, they believe the business has the potential to earn more income. They are considering three independent options for next summer to try to boost the company's income and give them more money for school next year. Details for the three options are presented below.

Option 1

The brothers could extend their hours of operation to take advantage of longer daylight hours in the summer. They believe there is sufficient demand to rent SUP boards seven hours a day. There would be no change to their selling price or their variable costs per unit, but Michael would want an additional $400 in salary to work in the evenings in the summer. Also, Nadja may not be available to work the extra hours so they will need to hire another summer student to work the extra two hours a day. They are not sure who they will be able to hire and if that person will fit with SUP Rides' culture.

Option 2

The brothers believe many people are reluctant to rent the boards because they have never tried the sport. If they include a lesson in the first 15 minutes of the rental time, they will be able to increase their price to $40 per hour. They believe this will increase the hours the boards are rented to six hours per day (without having to operate in the evenings). Variable costs per unit would stay the same. Michael would provide the lessons and the brothers agreed they would increase his monthly salary to $1,600 to recognize the extra work in providing lessons to their customers. Michael is happy to do this as he is planning on applying to teachers' college soon. Many of their customers are teenagers and the teaching experience will look good on his application.

Option 3

Instead of extending their hours or offering lessons, the brothers believe that advertising would bring more customers to their location on the beach and they would be able to increase the number of hours the boards are rented. They plan on spending $1,000 per month on advertising and promotion (including flyers, posters, and a website with basic information about SUP boards). Michael estimates this will allow them to rent the boards eight hours per day (assuming no change to the sales price, variable costs per unit, and other fixed costs). The other brothers are not convinced and think it is a lot of money to spend on advertising.

The brothers are not sure which option will result in higher monthly income and which is best for their company, or if they should keep things the way they are and be happy with their current income. They are also not sure about some of their estimates. For example, in Option 2, customers may not be willing to pay an extra $15 for a 15-minute lesson, especially if it is part of their hour of renting the boards. Maybe $35 would be more realistic initially, and they could always increase the price in the future if they did see a big increase in demand.

Required

Using a case format, prepare a report for the brothers outlining how the changing costs and volumes in each option would affect profit as well as the advantages and disadvantages of each option.

7.2 Jay-Dubs Disc Golf

Jonathan has a passion for disc golf. About 10 years ago, his very good friend Andy introduced him to the sport. Since then, the two of them have become masters of the sport. The two play several times a week and travel across the country seeking out new courses to practise their skills. One evening, while sitting around having dinner with their wives, the two men decided that they wanted to quit their jobs and open their own disc golf course. As the night went on, Jonathan's wife Sara (who is a chartered professional accountant) and Andy's wife Camille played along with the conversation, thinking that it was all an unrealistic dream. About a week later, the two men called a meeting together with their wives. They were serious about the idea, and had developed a plan to make their dream become a reality. Below is an account of the conversation:

Andy: Ladies, we have brought you here today to discuss our plans to start our very own disc golf course, "Jay-Dubs Disc Golf." We really think that this is going to work, but will need your support in order to make it happen.

Camille: Okay, let's hear it.

Andy: Jonathan and I have found the perfect place for the course. It is a large green piece of land that we are able to rent in Milton, Ontario. It is the perfect place for a course, because not only does it have a growing population, it is close to many larger cities, such as Mississauga, Toronto, Oakville, and Guelph. We spoke to the owners of the land, and they will make us pay rent only during the warmer months—from April to September. The rent they charge is $5,000 per month.

Sara: Okay, what about all the other costs?

Andy: I thought you might ask me that. We have drawn up a spreadsheet with all of the costs associated with the course (Exhibit 1).

Camille: How are you going to make money? All I see is a list of costs here. Every time we have gone to play disc golf, it has been free!

Jonathan: Good point; we are going to charge a fee for the course. We think that people will pay because there aren't really any disc golf courses in the area. The fee won't be much. We were thinking about $20 for 18 holes and $10 for 9 holes.

Sara: I don't mean to go all "accountant" on you, but it seems like you are going to need to sell a lot of rounds of golf in order to cover these costs. Also, what about making money to live? !

Jonathan: I knew you would ask about that, Sara. Andy and I will both quit our jobs and will start a painting business. When I was in college, I painted during the summers. It was great money and I loved it. We will paint during the warmer months part-time, and when it is cold and the course is closed, we will paint full-time. Don't worry, I know what you are going to ask next. We have analyzed the revenues and expenses associated with painting (Exhibit 2). Based on my previous painting experience, I know that the average painting job is 1,300 square feet. On an annual basis, we are forecasting that for every round of disc golf we sell, we should sell three painting jobs.

Sara: Okay, so how many rounds of disc golf and painting jobs do you need to sell in order to cover your fixed costs?

Andy: Oh, well, I guess we haven't got there yet. I'm not even sure how to figure that out, to be honest.

Camille: I'm concerned! Sara, to me it isn't just about covering the fixed costs; I'm worried about them making enough money for us to survive. I don't think I can support this unless Andy makes at least his current net salary of $60,000 per year.

Sara: Oh, good point, Camille, we need the equivalent of Jonathan's salary to survive too. He makes a net salary of $60,000 as well.

Jonathan: Well, we don't know how to figure this out. Sara, do you think you could run the numbers for us and let us know? I guess we need to know if this is feasible before we begin.

Sara: Okay, I will get on this soon, but please don't quit your job until we fully understand if this is feasible!

Required

Assume the role of Sara and prepare a report for Jonathan and Andy showing the level of sales required to cover their fixed costs (break even) in both businesses and the level of sales required to replace their existing incomes from both businesses. Assume a tax rate of 30%. Your report should include any qualitative factors that Jonathan and Andy should consider in their decision.

EXHIBIT 1 – COSTS ASSOCIATED WITH THE DISC GOLF BUSINESS

Cost	Amount	Comments
Land rent	$5,000 per month	Rent payments will be made in April to September
Equipment rent	$9,000 annually	
Property maintenance	$6,000 annually	

EXHIBIT 2 – REVENUES AND EXPENSES ASSOCIATED WITH THE PAINTING BUSINESS

Revenues/Expenses	Amount	Comments
Price charged per square foot:	$ 2.00	
Paint per square foot:	0.32	
Rollers (each)	1.49	4 rollers per job
Paint brushes	250.00	Annual cost
Other supplies	800.00	Annual cost
Depreciation—Vehicle	10,000.00	Annual cost
Advertising costs	2,000.00	Annual cost

7.3 Multiculture Bevco

Note: While this case is based on a real company, numbers and some company information have been changed to protect confidential information and to make the case appropriate for teaching purposes.

Multiculture Bevco (MBC) is a developer and marketer of high-quality, niche alcoholic beverage products. The Oakville, Ontario–based company developed and owns two vodka trademarks: Slava Ultra Premium Vodka and Zirkova Premium Vodka. The Slava and Zirkova trademarks, designs, and recipes are owned by MBC; however, the beverages are produced in Ukraine. The distillery is located in Zolotonosha, in the Cherkasy region, which was the birthplace of vodka during the Polish-Lithuanian empire. The vodka is currently sold in four provinces. MBC's vodka sales represent over 80% of alcoholic beverage imports from Ukraine to Canada.

John and Katherine started MBC in 2005 with the launch of Slava, and Zirkova followed a year later They are professional engineers who worked for a major distributor of consumer products after graduating from university, but they always dreamed of owning their own business. That dream was realized when they moved to Ukraine and founded a consulting firm which led them to discover the distillery in Zolotonosha. They saw the potential for niche vodkas specifically designed for how Canadians enjoy vodka but produced in a country that knows vodka. They both work full-time for MBC and currently have three employees. While MBC is profitable, as entrepreneurs their family income depends on MBC's income.

Slava is a martini or sipping vodka and is four times distilled and 12 times filtered, which puts it in the category of ultra premium. Zirkova is designed to make mixed drinks taste better; it is also four times distilled and is produced in the traditional method, without any additives. Both products have won gold medals at the San Francisco World Spirits Competition.

Required

John and Katherine are planning for next year and are considering two things. First, they would like to know how many units of Slava and Zirkova they need to sell next year to reach a target net income of $150,000 (ignore income taxes and duties). They are not sure how to calculate this because most of their fixed costs relate to both products. Second, they wonder how they could improve their costing system to help them make better decisions about their products and their company.

MBC's most recent income statement is provided in Exhibit 1. John and Katherine also estimate that 75% of variable manufacturing costs relate to Slava and they expect their current sales mix to stay the same next year.

Prepare a report for John and Katherine that addresses their questions.

EXHIBIT 1 – INCOME STATEMENT

MULTICULTURE BEVCO
Income Statement
Year Ended December 31, 20X2

Sales	$720,000
Cost of goods sold	312,000
Gross margin	408,000
Operating expenses	
Accounting and legal	23,600
Advertising and promotion	70,000
Bank charges	3,400
Commissions	40,000
Consulting	11,000
Depreciation	10,000
Insurance	9,000
Interest	6,000
Office and general administration	24,000
Rent	43,000
Salaries and benefits	95,000
Travel and vehicle	45,000
Utilities	5,000
Taxes and duties	8,000
Total operating expenses	393,000
Income	$ 15,000

Notes:

10% of cost of goods sold includes fixed manufacturing overhead.

All operating expenses are fixed except commissions.

$35,000 of commissions relates to Slava and $5,000 relates to Zirkova.

The 20X2 sales revenue represented sales of $400,000 for Slava and $320,000 for Zirkova. Slava sells for $10 per bottle and Zirkova sells for $4 per bottle.

These are sales to the various liquor boards in each province. For example, in Ontario, sales are to the LCBO, which then marks up the product for sale to the consumer in its retail outlets.

7.4 Quench Their Thirst

Quench Their Thirst (QTT) is a not-for-profit organization located in Vancouver. It makes and sells bottled water, and for every bottle sold, it puts $0.25 toward providing clean drinking water to those in need. QTT works with another not-for-profit organization, Clean Water Aid (CWA), whose mission is to provide clean drinking water. Once CWA identifies an area of significant need, there are various ways that it provides aid. For example, in some cases, it donates or purchases equipment that will clean the water to be safe for consumption. In other cases, CWA ships water directly to the identified areas. CWA provides a detailed audited report annually of the aid provided to various affected areas. Once a year, the founder of CWA travels to the areas that have received support to ensure that the resources are being used effectively.

QTT has been in operation for just over a year. The two founders, Alex and Yim-Ling Huang, have been married for just over three years. In order be able to devote themselves full-time to QTT, they live in Alex's parents' basement. His parents are very generous and do not require any rent payments, but the couple is considering moving out soon. However, in order to do so, they will need to start to take more salary out of QTT. As it stands right now, the couple is paid a combined salary of $25,000 from QTT, which is the maximum amount of cash that is available for withdrawal. Alex and Yim-Ling are wondering by how much they would have to increase sales in order to be able to withdraw a combined salary of $80,000. As they sat down to discuss whether it is feasible, they realized that they aren't even sure how many bottles of water they sold this year! The only thing they know is that, for every bottle of water they sell as a single bottle, they sell two cases of 24 bottles of water.

In order to get some help, Alex and Yim-Ling have asked for your assistance. You are a new Certified Professional Accountant and have agreed to act as a treasurer on the QTT's board of directors. In order to help Alex and Yim-Ling with their request, you have asked them to provide you with a detailed list of their revenues and expenses (which they provided in Exhibit 1). In addition, Alex mentioned to you that the variable costs associated with packaging a 24-bottle case are $0.07. In addition to selling water bottles, Alex and Yim-Ling have considered selling merchandise to promote QTT. Many customers are excited about the organization because they feel they are helping those in need with every purchase they make. Alex and Yim-Ling have done some research with respect to selling T-shirts and have provided their preliminary research in Exhibit 2.

Required

Write a report responding to the couple's questions. If they decide to pursue the sale of T-shirts, how many bottles of water, cases of water, and T-shirts would they have to sell to achieve the desired level of salary? Yim-Ling stated that she felt that for every water bottle they sold, they could sell 10 T-shirts. They would like your report to comment on two scenarios: one that includes the sale of T-shirts and one that does not.

EXHIBIT 1 – SUMMARY OF REVENUE AND EXPENSES

Revenue

Water bottle sales	$3,222,000

Expenses

Variable costs	2,689,050
Selling expenses	496,550
Taxes	10,920
Total expenses	3,196,520
Revenue over Expenses	$ 25,480

Notes:

Selling price, single water bottle	$1.50
Selling price, 24-bottle case	$9.99

EXHIBIT 2 – ALEX AND YIM-LING'S NOTES REGARDING T-SHIRT SALES

Selling price	$19.99
Variable costs	$ 8.00

7.5 Arctic Candy Company

Contributed by
Jo-Anne Ryan CPA, CA, PhD
Assistant Professor, Laurentian University, Barrie

Chuck Sweet and his sister Kay grew up watching their grandmother make the best chocolates at Christmas using an old family recipe. They have decided that it is time to mass-market the chocolates, expecting them to be especially popular around the holiday season. They have already chosen a name for their new company: the Arctic Candy Company (ACC).

ACC's owners have come to you and asked for help in determining the feasibility of their new venture. They would like you to prepare a report that incorporates a break-even analysis and any other analysis you deem necessary given the information provided. You should also include a qualitative discussion of the risks and opportunities of the new venture. The information they provided is found in Exhibit 1.

Required

Prepare the report for Chuck and Kay, showing your calculations.

EXHIBIT 1 – INFORMATION PROVIDED BY THE ARCTIC CANDY COMPANY

- » It is estimated that approximately $100 million is spent annually by consumers on chocolate worldwide.

- » ACC believes that with its superior chocolate recipe, it can obtain somewhere between 0.5% and 2% of the worldwide chocolate market. Based on its market research, ACC expects the probabilities of the market potential for ACC to be as follows:

  - 0.5% of worldwide market – 15%

  - 1% of worldwide market – 60%

  - 2% of worldwide market – 25%

- » ACC intends to sell each box of chocolates for $10.00 to retailers.

- » Direct materials are expected to be $2 per box and direct labour $1. The packaging of the chocolates is expected to cost $1.50 per box.

- » ACC will incur fixed expenses of $500,000 annually. This includes the rent on a building located in the downtown core and a fixed distribution fee to retailers.

- » ACC will not be tax exempt. It has a tax rate of 30%. In order to make the project feasible, ACC wants to ultimately make an after-tax annual profit of $130,000.

7.6 The Sweetest Tooth

Janelle Veenstra faces some serious issues with her business, The Sweetest Tooth, that she started only a short three months ago. She has recently come to you for some advice on how to make her business profitable before it is too late. Below are the notes from your first meeting with Janelle.

» Janelle started her business in March 20X3. After travelling through the United States, she enjoyed visiting several specialty dessert shops, which primarily focused on gourmet cupcakes. After speaking with several shop owners, she decided to open a gourmet cupcake shop of her own, located in Mississauga, Ontario.

» The store is a place for customers to buy a cupcake and a tea or coffee. There are also a few tables and chairs for customers to sit and enjoy their cupcake. Janelle does all of the baking in her home during the evenings. Eventually, Janelle plans to move to a location where she can perform the baking on-site so she doesn't have to use her home.

» Beginning in February 20X3, Janelle leased the premises where her shop is located. The shop is next to a busy shopping centre and therefore she pays a premium for rent. Her monthly rent is $2,200. A list of other business expenses are in Exhibit 1.

» Janelle buys her baking and store supplies from a large wholesaler located in Mississauga. She has provided you with two months (April and May) of receipts of purchases (Exhibit 1).

» On average, Janelle has to throw out about a dozen cupcakes a week as they go stale. Other than that, there is no other waste.

» Janelle charges $3.50 per cupcake and $1.50 for a tea or a coffee. There are no other products that are sold in her store.

» The monthly sales receipts are shown for April and May (Exhibit 2).

Janelle is worried. She has found that she doesn't have enough money in a month to cover her living expenses (Exhibit 3). She recently had to borrow money from her parents in order to pay her rent for her apartment.

Required

Prepare a memo to Janelle to help her to understand why she doesn't have enough money to meet her monthly living expenses. Provide Janelle with some suggestions in order to improve the profitability of her business and strategies to ensure she meets all of her monthly obligations.

EXHIBIT 1 – THE SWEETEST TOOTH BUSINESS EXPENSES

The Sweetest Tooth's Monthly Business Expenses May 20X3	
Rent	$ 2,200.00
Electricity	146.50
Gas	86.00
Phone	36.00
Internet	87.00
Supplies (see receipt)	631.12
Insurance	180.00
Fixtures rentals	1,100.00
Total	**$4,466.62**

Receipt of Purchases April 1, 20X3		
Item	Quantity	Total Price
McBakes all-purpose flour	4	$ 26.68
McBakes white sugar	4	34.60
McBakes icing sugar	4	42.60
McBakes baking soda	5	39.90
McBakes baking powder	3	11.00
McBakes vanilla	5	22.75
McBakes food colouring	4	39.88
Clucks Eggs	10	49.70
All salt	1	12.95
Lacter milk	15	70.05
Fats full butter	5	19.95
Fats cream cheese	3	17.01
McCoffee grinds	4	19.94
Spots tea bags	2	23.90
Plastic cups	4	42.68
Napkins	4	39.96
Paper bags	4	47.80
Total		**$561.35**

EXHIBIT 1 – THE SWEETEST TOOTH BUSINESS EXPENSES (*CONTINUED*)

Receipt of Purchases May 1, 20X3		
Item	Quantity	Total Price
McBakes all-purpose flour	5	$ 33.35
McBakes white sugar	4	34.60
McBakes icing sugar	3	31.95
McBakes baking soda	6	47.88
McBakes baking powder	4	14.67
McBakes vanilla	6	27.30
McBakes food colouring	6	59.82
Clucks eggs	10	49.70
All salt	1	12.95
Lacter milk	18	84.06
Fats full butter	4	15.96
Fats cream cheese	4	22.68
McCoffee grinds	4	29.91
Spots tea bags	3	35.85
Plastic cups	4	42.68
Napkins	4	39.96
Paper bags	4	47.80
Total		**$631.12**

EXHIBIT 2 – MONTHLY SALES RECEIPTS

Detailed Sales Log - Number Sold				
	March	**April**	**May**	**Total**
Cupcakes	1,104	1,121	1,225	3,450
Coffee/Tea	64	76	84	224
Total	1,168	1,197	1,309	3,674

EXHIBIT 3 – JANELLE'S MONTHLY PERSONAL EXPENSES

Janelle's Monthly Personal Expenses May 20X3	
Rent	$1,400.00
Electricity	55.78
Cellphone	332.56
Internet and cable	136.00
Food	556.00
Fuel	240.00
Insurance	120.00
Clothes	586.00
Entertainment	758.00
Total expenses	**$4,184.34**

Chapter 8: Variable Costing

8.1 Double Edge Ltd.

Contributed by
Amy Lunov CMA
Lecturer, University of Regina, Regina

Double Edge Ltd. is a privately owned company providing residential housing. It manufactures modular homes at a factory and then ships them to the customer's premises. These types of houses are seen as a quality alternative to houses built on-site. The company provides several base models and customers can enhance the homes based on their individual preferences for cabinets, flooring, moulding, fixtures, and so on.

These homes provide buyers with several advantages, including lower purchase costs than on-site houses, the ability to customize based on individual preferences, ease of relocation if necessary, and lower operating costs. Modular homes also save buyers time, because they can typically be built and delivered in two to three months, compared with several months to have a house built on-site.

Double Edge's factory and administration office is in Springfield. It recently updated and expanded its operations, enabling it to produce almost twice as many units as before. Currently the company employs 325 people.

The company operates with a dealer network throughout Canada. The dealers interact with the customers, take the orders, show customers the show homes, and deal with after-sales services such as warranty or resale. Double Edge Ltd. produces show homes that it keeps on inventory as well as homes ordered by the dealers for their customers. Houses come in four main widths: 16 feet, 20 feet, 22 feet, and 24 feet.

The company's directors have decided to use variable costing to better understand their business. They are aware that in some companies, managers manipulate profits by overproducing units to increase operating profit. In the modular home business, the overproduction of units is not favourable to the company. Since it is not possible to manipulate profits with variable costing, the directors have asked you to prepare a variable costing income statement and an absorption costing income statement for the company for the last quarter of the year. They would like to know what the main differences are between the statements, including what the per unit cost would be under each scenario, and a reconciliation between the variable cost net income and the absorption cost net income. Finally, they would like you to provide the minimum dollar amount of sales required in order to cover the period costs. Additional information from the fourth quarter is in Exhibit 1 to help you in your analysis.

Required

Prepare the following information as required by Double Edge:

1. A variable costing income statement and an absorption costing income statement
2. An analysis of the differences between the two approaches, including what the per unit cost would be under both approaches
3. A reconciliation of absorption costing net income and variable costing net income
4. An analysis of the minimum dollar amount of sales required in order to cover the period costs

EXHIBIT 1 – SELECTED FINANCIAL INFORMATION FOR DOUBLE EDGE LTD.

Units produced	460
Units sold	460
Average price per unit	$ 143,000
Direct materials	$13,800,000
Direct labour	$18,400,000
Variable manufacturing overhead	$ 9,200,000
Variable selling and administration expenses	$ 2,300,000
Fixed selling and administration expenses	$ 6,900,000
Fixed manufacturing overhead	$ 9,200,000

Chapter 9: Budgeting

9.1 Allure Canada

Allure is a Japanese automotive manufacturer that specializes in family sedans, trucks, and SUVs. In the 1980s, Allure saw a great opportunity to sell its vehicles in North America. As a result, in 1981 Allure started Allure Canada, a wholly owned subsidiary of Allure Japan. Since 1981, the Allure brand has become very popular in Canada. Many published consumer reports have referred to the Allure sedan as the safest family car on the road in Canada. The Allure vehicles are known for lasting several years and many families use theirs for more than 10 years. Other than regular maintenance, Allure vehicles generally do not require major repair within the first five years. Since the expansion into North America, Allure has subsidiaries all over the world, including several European countries.

In 1981, when Allure first started its operations in Canada, 100% of the manufacturing was in Japan. In 1990, Allure opened its first manufacturing facility outside of Japan in Ontario. The Ontario plant would be responsible for manufacturing all of the vehicles for the Canadian market. The majority of the parts are manufactured in-house or outsourced to a third party in Canada. In order to maintain control, Allure Japan shipped all spark plugs (an important part of each engine) to the Canadian subsidiary. Allure Japan has a very efficient inventory control system and traditionally has not involved the Canadian division in deciding how many spark plugs would be shipped to Canada each month. Allure Japan always ships enough spark plugs to Canada every month to ensure that 50% of the next month's demand is met. (Each vehicle requires four spark plugs.) During 20X2, Japan suffered from a very significant earthquake that caused severe damage across the country, including the destruction of Allure's manufacturing plant. On December 15, Allure Japan notified the Canadian subsidiary that it would not be shipping any more spark plugs to Canada for at least one year.

On December 15, Allure Canada's Vice President of Operations, Elena Zajac, received the notice that Allure Japan would not ship any more spark plugs for a year, and she called an emergency meeting. At the meeting were the production manager, Alain Boulerice, and you, the cost accountant. Elena has asked that you review sales forecasts (Exhibit 1) for the following year, and determine the monthly amounts of spark plugs to purchase and the cash requirements to do so. As soon as the earthquake hit Japan, Alain was worried that something like this could happen. Alain has received quotes from two suppliers (Exhibit 2) and brought them to the meeting for your review.

Required

Elena has asked you to state which one of the suppliers' offers you would recommend and mention your potential concerns. Write a report to Elena, keeping in mind that Allure Canada has a limited number of spark plugs in inventory.

EXHIBIT 1 – SALES FORECAST

Planned Car Sales Per Month (In Units)

Jan.	Feb.	Mar.	April	May	June
6,500	5,500	4,000	4,200	4,500	8,000

July	Aug.	Sept.	Oct.	Nov.	Dec.
8,500	9,950	9,000	9,000	5,500	2,000

EXHIBIT 2 – SUPPLIER QUOTES

Quote #1

To: Allure Canada
From: Walks Automotive
Re: Spark Plug Purchase

Walks Automotive is a wholly owned subsidiary of TCI Automotive (a German automotive manufacturer). Walks Automotive has operated under the control of TCI Automotive for 20 years. The company manufactures various engine parts such as cylinders, pistons, spark plugs, and valves. These parts are primarily manufactured for TCI Automotive, Canada. However, Walks Automotive has recently expanded and also supplies other automotive manufacturers in Canada. Walks Automotive makes top quality a priority and will only provide top-quality products.

Pricing: $24.99 (per unit)

Guarantee: Each spark plug comes with a one-year guarantee. The guarantee period begins when the vehicle is delivered to the customer. The dealer will be responsible for replacing any defective spark plug and filing a claim with Walks Automotive for reimbursement.

Delivery Terms: Each shipment will be delivered within 30 days of purchase. If the delivery date is not met, Walks Automotive will deliver the shipment free of charge.

Payment Terms: Due on delivery

Quote #2

SPARKS INC.

Sparks Inc. specializes in the manufacturing of spark plugs. Sparks Inc. is based in Florida, but ships to anywhere in North America. Sparks Inc. has been in operation for three years.

Pricing: $13.99 (CDN dollars, per unit)

Payment Terms: 5% of the outstanding balance when the product is delivered, 30% in the following month, and the balance two months after the purchase is made

Money Back Guarantee: Sparks Inc. will replace any malfunctioning spark plug, free of charge, to its customers. Upon initial testing of the engine, if the spark plug does not work, Sparks Inc. will replace the spark plug. (Note: This offer is valid within 3 months of purchase.)

Delivery Terms: Sparks Inc. aims to ensure that each order placed is delivered within 15 days of purchase.

9.2 Change Purse Inc.

Contributed by
Mary M. Oxner PhD, CA, CFA
Associate Professor, Gerald Schwartz School of Business, St. Francis Xavier University, Antigonish

Change Purse Inc. is a small business that is planned to be located in a small Nova Scotia town. The town was incorporated in 1889 and, like many communities in Nova Scotia, it prides itself on being able to offer a unique quality of life to its citizens. Much of its history recognizes the importance of individuals, family, and community. The town's council has emphasized attracting small businesses to the area based on its quality of life.

Bethany Ng, the owner of Change Purse Inc., believes that there is a market for handbags in the town and surrounding area. Bethany just received her degree in design from a provincial college of art and design and thought about starting the business during the last year of her academic program. Bethany believes that her unique approach to design and her use of "green" materials in the production of the handbags will attract potential customers. Her assessment of the market demand included a phone survey of a random sampling of town residents, an analysis of population data retrieved from the Statistics Canada website, and an assessment of the availability of competitive products in the town and surrounding area. Following her market assessment, Bethany incorporated a business with the intention of opening a small location on July 1, 20X3, on the town's main street, where she would manufacture and sell a variety of bags, from diaper bags to evening bags. All the materials will be sourced from local suppliers and the manufacturing will be done by Bethany.

Although handbags represent a difficult market to conquer, Bethany expects sales to be reasonably strong. She spent the last few months working on a business plan and she has considered various aspects of her business model. Handbag sales are anticipated to come from the Internet (15%), mail orders over the phone (15%), and walk-ins to the store (70%). All on-line and mail-order sales are to be paid by credit card and the in-store sales are anticipated to be paid by cash (10%), debit card (30%), and credit card (60%). Bethany has made an arrangement with a local financial institution such that the debit processing will be done the same day but the credit card processing will be done on the last day of the month for the entire month's credit card sales. The cost of credit card processing is a fee of 5% of the total amount processed, while the debit card processing is covered by her monthly business banking fees.

The manufacturing process takes approximately two months. To take advantage of fabric and material purchase discounts, Bethany plans to buy the material for the year in January and February (50% in each month) and she will do all the manufacturing herself. Because Bethany will be buying material in July for 20X3, she will need to purchase and pay for all the material at once to get the discount. The cost of the materials will vary depending on the type of bag, with costs approximating $20, $10, $10, and $50 per bag for diaper, shopping, school, and evening bags, respectively; the cost includes the discount for buying in January and February. Bethany has already contributed $1,000 in cash when incorporating the business; therefore, she expects to have access to the $1,000 in cash that she contributed and a $10,000 line of credit (5% annual interest cost) that she has already secured from her financial institution and from which she can borrow in $1,000 increments. The anticipated sales price, volume, and pattern are presented in Exhibit 1 and the expected monthly expenses are presented in Exhibit 2; monthly expenses are paid in cash in the month incurred.

Required

Bethany Ng has come to you, a professional accountant, for advice concerning her proposed business plan. In particular, Bethany wants help in budgeting her monthly financial resources and projecting her potential monthly income. Write a report to Bethany.

EXHIBIT 1 – ANTICIPATED SALES PRICE, VOLUME, AND PATTERN FOR 20X4*

Product Type	Selling Price	Sales Volume	Sales Pattern
Diaper bags	$150	100	50% in December, 25% in April, and 25% in July
Shopping bags	$ 40	250	10% per month except December and January
School bags	$ 40	150	90% in August and 10% in January
Evening bags	$175	25	100% in December

*Note: 20X3 sales are expected to be 30% of the 20X4 monthly sales levels.

EXHIBIT 2 – ANTICIPATED MONTHLY EXPENSES FOR 20X4**

Type of Expense	Cost
Rent (including heat and electricity)	$1,000
Office supplies	$ 100
Phone and Internet	$ 200
Postage and courier	$ 100
Marketing and public relations	$ 300
Banking fees	$ 100

**Note: 20X3 expenses are expected to be the same as 20X4 expenses; however, marketing and public relations fees are expected to be double the 20X4 level in 20X3.

Chapter 10: Variances

10.1 Hook Clothing Ltd.

Josh turned off his computer after an afternoon of gathering data. He was scheduled to meet with his business partner, Athina, tomorrow to review last month's performance and he wanted to make sure he was fully prepared for the meeting.

Josh and Athina are co-owners of Hook Clothing Ltd., a manufacturer of T-shirts, sweatshirts, and other items such as hats, gloves, and scarves. Their approach to design is unique in that they partner with emerging artists to promote their work by printing it on their clothing. The company prides itself on the artistic nature of its products, believing it is selling more than just clothing; it is selling wearable art. The uniqueness and quality of its products has allowed it to set its sales prices at the higher end of the market.

Hook's products are sold on the company's website and in specialty clothing stores across the country. While sales overall have been increasing in recent years, T-shirt sales have grown the most and Hook has needed to hire additional staff in order to produce enough T-shirts to meet demand. Last month, Hook produced and sold 3,500 T-shirts.

Josh has summarized information related to the production of T-shirts in Exhibit 1 and has asked you to help him finish his analysis for his meeting tomorrow with Athina. Josh wants to have all the appropriate calculations done before his meeting with Athina and also to have some explanations for her for the variances and what they reveal about Hook's production process.

Required

Help Josh get ready for his meeting with Athina by calculating variances and brainstorm potential reasons for the variances as well as their implications for Hook Clothing Ltd.

EXHIBIT 1 – INFORMATION ON T-SHIRT PRODUCTION

Direct Materials—Fabric		Direct Materials—Ink	
Actual price per m²	$10.00	Actual price per litre	$3.50
Standard price per m²	$11.00	Standard price per litre	$3.00
Actual m² purchased and used	1,100	Actual litres used and purchased	45
Standard m² of fabric allowed per unit	0.3	Standard litres of ink allowed per unit	0.014

10.2 Clear Water Containers Ltd.

Contributed by
Glen Stanger
Instructor, Douglas College, New Westminster

James Virani, the president of Clear Water Containers, started contemplating the first budget variance report he had just received (Exhibit 1). It seemed to present him with more questions than answers. He knew that production had exceeded expectations for the month and he had expected production costs to be higher. However, he couldn't tell what had caused the variances from budget, especially since some of the costs were actually lower than budgeted. A couple of minutes later, he called the company's new controller, Patti Lee.

Patti saw the call display on her phone and got nervous right away. She had thought it might not be a good idea to send such a high-level variance report without investigating the variances further, and wondered if that was why Mr. Virani was calling. Two minutes later, she had her answer: the president scheduled a meeting with her for the next day and she was to bring information that provided more details about the variances and who was responsible.

Creating the variance report was Patti's first innovation since starting with Clear Water Containers two months ago. She was excited to join this new and growing Calgary-based manufacturing company, which makes plastic containers for the consumer water filtration industry. The company found a competitive advantage by producing a high-quality product that can be quickly made in designs specified by the water filtration companies.

Patti gathered the information in several exhibits to use as the source for her work. Exhibits 2 and 3 show unit standard and actual costs, respectively. Exhibit 4 shows overhead costs; note that fixed overhead is allocated based on direct labour hours. She also grabbed the company's organization chart, shown in Exhibit 5.

Required

Assume the role of Patti and do the following to prepare for your meeting with the president.

(a) Create a new report, similar to Exhibit 1 but with the following column headings: Actual Results, Flexible Budget Variances, Flexible Budget, Sales Volume Variances, and Static Budget.

(b) Prepare a flexible-budget variance analysis for direct materials, direct labour, variable manufacturing overhead, and fixed manufacturing overhead. In your analysis, break each flexible budget variance for these costs into two components. For example, fixed manufacturing overhead will be presented in two parts: budget variance and production-volume variance.

(c) Identify the likely manager responsible for each account and prepare a static budget variance report organized by responsibility. Remember that for overhead there are often multiple managers involved because overhead includes so many different costs.

EXHIBIT 1 – STATIC BUDGET VARIANCE REPORT

	Actual Results	Static Budget Variances	Static Budget
Units produced and sold	72,000	8,000	64,000
Sales revenue	$1,152,000	$ 96,000	$1,056,000
Variable costs:			
Direct materials	216,000	(36,800)	179,200
Direct labour	360,000	24,000	384,000
Variable manufacturing	57,600	9,600	67,200
Other variable costs	242,000	24,000	266,000
Contribution margin	276,400	116,800	159,600
Fixed manufacturing costs	75,000	(3,000)	72,000
Operating income	$ 201,400	$113,800	$ 87,600

EXHIBIT 2 – UNIT STANDARD COSTS

	Quantity Standard	Price Standard	Standard Price per Unit
Sales revenue			$16.50
Variable manufacturing costs:			
Direct materials	2 kg/unit	$1.40/kg	$2.80
Direct labour	0.5 hr/unit	$12.00/hr	$6.00
Other variable manufacturing	1.0 hr/unit	$1.05/hr	$1.05

EXHIBIT 3 – UNIT ACTUAL COSTS

	Actual Quantity	Actual Price	Actual Price per Unit
Sales revenue			$16.00
Variable manufacturing costs:			
Direct materials	3 kg/unit	$1.00/kg	$3.00
Direct labour	0.4 hr/unit	$12.50/hr	$5.00
Other variable manufacturing	0.8 hr/unit	$1.00/hr	$0.80

EXHIBIT 4 – OVERHEAD COSTS

	Actual	Static Budget
Variable manufacturing overhead accounts:		
Maintenance	$ 9,000	$12,000
Batch set-up	15,300	15,900
Contracted cleaning	13,900	17,800
Indirect materials	5,100	4,900
Inspection	10,200	12,400
Utilities	4,100	4,200
Total variable manufacturing overhead	$57,600	$67,200
Fixed manufacturing overhead accounts:		
Depreciation, factory	$12,500	$12,500
Indirect labour	13,200	11,900
Property taxes, factory	1,100	1,100
Contracted maintenance	10,700	7,700
Insurance, factory	2,100	2,100
Equipment rental	35,400	36,700
Total fixed manufacturing overhead	$75,000	$72,000

EXHIBIT 5 – CLEAR WATER CONTAINERS ORGANIZATION CHART

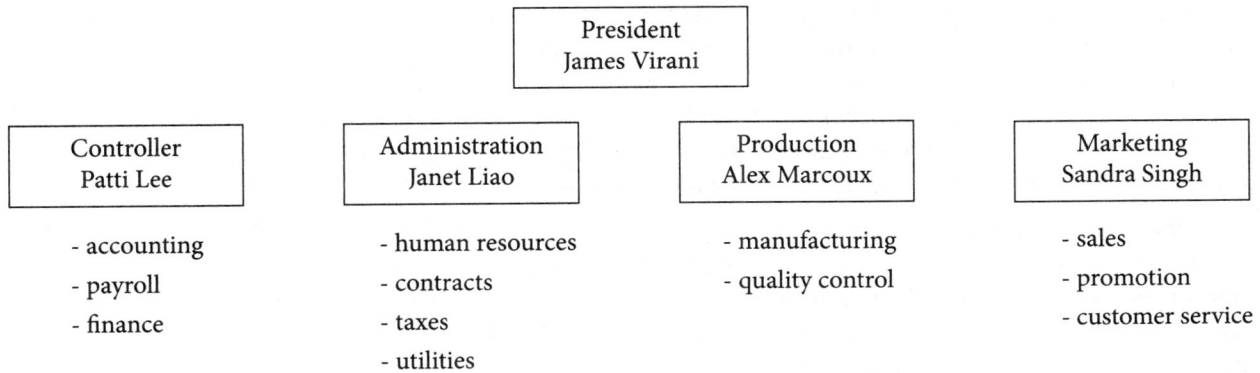

```
                        ┌──────────────────┐
                        │   President      │
                        │   James Virani   │
                        └──────────────────┘

┌──────────────┐   ┌──────────────────┐   ┌──────────────┐   ┌──────────────┐
│  Controller  │   │  Administration  │   │  Production  │   │  Marketing   │
│  Patti Lee   │   │   Janet Liao     │   │ Alex Marcoux │   │ Sandra Singh │
└──────────────┘   └──────────────────┘   └──────────────┘   └──────────────┘
```

- accounting	- human resources	- manufacturing	- sales
- payroll	- contracts	- quality control	- promotion
- finance	- taxes		- customer service
	- utilities		

Chapter 11: Performance Measurement

11.1 Sohni Company

Sohni Company is a retailer with operations across Canada. Sohni is divided into four divisions (Western, Prairie, Central, and Eastern). Each division is treated as an investment centre in that it has responsibility for its income as well as the capital invested in the division. A consolidated income statement for 20X3 is given in Exhibit 1 and highlights of a segmented balance sheet are in Exhibit 2.

It's Maelle Stewart's first year as president of Sohni. Maelle is a certified accountant and, while she has never been in charge of such a large organization, she has extensive experience at several smaller Canadian firms.

Sohni currently uses return on investment (ROI) to evaluate the four divisions. Maelle is aware of the challenges of using ROI and wonders if there is a better way to measure divisional performance. Managers of the four divisions each have projects they are considering for 20X4. Exhibit 3 lists the projects' required investment as well as the estimated increase in operating income from the projects.

A management team meeting is scheduled next week and items on the agenda include the divisional performance in 20X3 and the planned investments in the divisions for 20X4. Also, the Eastern division has always been the poorest-performing division and the previous president had often questioned whether the division should be dropped. This issue will likely resurface at the meeting. The divisional managers will be at the meeting and Maelle wants to make sure she is prepared. She will need a report that outlines the ROI in 20X3 for each division as well as the effect on the division's ROI if the projects are accepted for 20X4. She also needs to think about how to deal with the issue of dropping the Eastern division.

Finally, Maelle remembers learning about residual income as another way to evaluate the performance of investment centres when she was studying for her accounting designation but she has never had the opportunity to use this tool. She wants to look into this for the meeting and see what effect residual income would have on the divisional performance last year and the decision to invest in the divisions next year. She gets to work right away and starts by finding the following information:

» 20X3 revenue was $11 million in the Western division, $3 million in the Prairie division, $9 million in the Central division, and $2 million in the Eastern division.

» Variable costs are assumed to be 20% of revenue.

» Fixed costs were divided among the divisions as follows: $3.5 million (Western), $800,000 (Prairie), $3 million (Central), and $600,000 (Eastern).

» The required rate of return for all divisions is 10%.

Required

Assume the role of Maelle and prepare a report that addresses the issues outlined above.

EXHIBIT 1 – CONSOLIDATED INCOME STATEMENT

SOHNI COMPANY

Consolidated Income Statement

Year Ended December 31, 20X3

$000'S

Revenue	25,000
Expenses	12,900
Operating income	12,100
Interest (12%)	1,452
Income before income taxes	10,648
Income taxes (35%)	3,727
Net income	6,921

EXHIBIT 2 – HIGHLIGHTS OF THE SEGMENTED BALANCE SHEET

SOHNI COMPANY

Highlights of the Segmented Balance Sheet

as at December 31, 20X3

$000's

	Western	Prairie	Central	Eastern	Total
Total assets	15,000	3,500	10,000	2,000	30,500
Total liabilities	5,250	1,575	4,400	840	12,065
Total shareholders' equity	9,750	1,925	5,600	1,160	18,435

EXHIBIT 3 – POTENTIAL CAPITAL EXPENDITURES FOR 20X4

	Western	Prairie	Central	Eastern	Total
Increase in operating income	400	200	500	300	1,400
Investment required	3,200	800	1,000	1,200	6,200

Chapter 12: Relevant Costs

12.1 NutriCrisp Incorporated

Contributed by
Jo-Anne Ryan CPA, CA, PhD
Assistant Professor, Laurentian University, Barrie

Lillian Crisp incorporated NutriCrisp two years ago, hoping to eventually tap into the lucrative health cereal market. Located in southwestern Ontario, NutriCrisp Inc. has yet to start selling any cereal, but Lillian has completed test production and researched the cereal industry.

Lillian has taken her grandmother's secret recipe for all-natural cereals and has developed three varieties: banana/chocolate/oat, strawberry/cream/nut, and papaya/plum/wheat bran. All cereals will be manufactured in a similar way, will use the same production facilities, and will have almost identical cost structures.

Recognizing that she doesn't have an adequate background in accounting, Lillian has hired you to help her. The data she collected are in Exhibit 1.

Required

In a report to Lillian, use the data that she has collected and calculate her anticipated break-even point. In addition, Lillian would like you to address any factors that may impact your calculations and provide details that support your calculations and assumptions. In this report, you should evaluate the information she has provided you with and address any concerns you may have, including marketing or strategic concerns.

EXHIBIT 1 – INFORMATION COLLECTED BY LILLIAN

» The Canadian cereal market is a multi-billion-dollar industry, with average annual revenues approximating $456 million. Smaller companies tend to be more profitable than larger companies.

» Lillian expects to lease space at a manufacturing facility for $10,000 per month. This includes the use of its machinery for production.

» The cost of the raw materials is the most expensive part of the manufacturing process. Lillian estimates that each box will result in raw material costs of $1.45 (including packaging). This is higher than the industry average but is the result of the low production volume she is estimating, and the higher quality of ingredients being used in the cereal.

» Lillian is estimating that her fixed administrative expenses will approximate $120,000 annually, excluding any salary she would pay herself.

» Production labour is considered variable in this industry and is estimated at $0.50 per box.

» Lillian is targeting health food stores and upscale grocery stores and is expecting to charge the stores $4.20 per box with a target retail price to consumers of $4.99.

» At a minimum, Lillian believes she can sell about 5,500 boxes per month in her first three months, and then about 8,500 boxes per month thereafter. Based on her research, she believes that she can actually sell 7,000 per month in her first three months, and then 11,000 boxes per month thereafter.

» If her cereal takes off quickly, a lofty but not unrealistic target would be monthly sales of 19,000 boxes.

» Lillian would like an after-tax target profit for NutriCrisp of $60,000 as this would allow her to pay herself a small salary. You are assuming a tax rate of 30% in your calculations.

12.2 Jewel of the Nile

Contributed by
Frank Saccucci
Instructor, MacEwan University, Edmonton

Upon graduation from the Northern University School of Business, Janelle Kawapit launched an on-line jewellery business called Jewel of the Nile. In Janelle's last year of her business program, there was a mandatory course called Small Business Management. One of the requirements in this course was a group assignment to build a business plan on any start-up venture. It was at this time that she convinced the other two group members, Kevin and Philippe, to build a business plan for an on-line jewellery business. Kevin, an accounting major, and Philippe, a marketing major, later became business partners when Jewel of the Nile was launched.

The three knew upfront that there wasn't anything unique about an on-line jewellery business and that their business could easily be another "marble in the marble jar." The unique features they incorporated into the business plan and brought forward into the launch were as follows:

1. The jewellery would be designed by women for women. Women could submit their designs on-line according to a template design chart available on the Jewel of the Nile website.

2. The original designer would receive $10 for every piece sold on-line.

3. Jewel of the Nile would donate 10% of the selling price to charities providing services to women in need in less-developed countries.

4. The jewellery manufacturing will be done by qualified artisans and not mass-produced abroad. On average, Jewel of the Nile will be charged $50 per jewellery piece by the qualified craftsperson.

5. For a personal touch, shipping would be from the artisan directly to the client. This would come at a $10 cost to Jewel of the Nile.

The business was run out of one of the partners' 900-sq.-ft. (83-m^2) condo, of which 90 sq. ft (8.3 m^2) was allocated to the jewellery business. Ten percent of the condo's annual carrying cost was expensed through Jewel of the Nile. The 10% of property tax, insurance, utilities, mortgage interest, and condo fees amounted to $1,700 per year. The company also hired a web designer at a cost of $200 a month, the company's tax return was prepared by a public accountant for $1,000 a year, and there was $500 of amortization of laptop and printers.

The three partners were feeling a bit discouraged after their first year of operation. With an average selling price of $109 per piece of jewellery, they just reached the break-even point. They realized that break-even represented only 20% of capacity. None of the partners drew a salary from Jewel of the Nile and therefore they still had to work at entry-level management positions. On top of that, each partner was devoting about 10 hours a week to the business.

Just as they were about to give up, a jewellery design company called Carolina's Design and Fashion from Denmark contacted them and offered to purchase 400 pieces at $89 each. The pieces would be sold only in Denmark. If the order was accepted, the $10 fee for normal shipping would not apply and they would incur only a lump-sum shipping cost of $800 to Denmark. The three partners met for coffee the following night to discuss the offer. Two of the partners were not excited about the offer given that they had just reached break-even and now were expected to give a large price discount on this volume purchase. They didn't know what to do and turned to you for help.

Required

Write a report to Janelle, Kevin, and Philippe advising them whether to take on the order from Denmark. Before you tackle the question of what they should do, ask yourself what does 20% capacity represent in units and how much profit is to be made on the special order? Give thought to both analytical and qualitative information, such as the fact that no salary has been drawn to date.

12.3 Fit Apparel

Fit Apparel (FA) sells high-quality workout clothing across Canada and the United States. FA is a private company owned by two sisters, Trina and Cora Smith. Ten years ago, the sisters decided to turn their lives around and get healthy. This involved a strict eating plan and an even stricter workout regimen. One thing that they both found motivating was feeling good at the gym, including wearing stylish clothes. The sisters decided to begin manufacturing and selling premium-priced workout apparel to both men and women. After many bumps along the road, 10 years later FA operates as a successful and extremely profitable business.

Fit Apparel doesn't have physical stores. You must purchase the clothing from an independent consultant. The independent consultants are experts on the product and are very passionate about what they do. It is the role of the independent consultant to market the product. The most common way that this is done is usually by hosting in-home parties. The consultant will visit a customer's home, and showcase the top-selling apparel items to a group of friends. There are many different incentives for the consultants, which make their job very lucrative; over 80% of the consultants earn more than $130,000 per year. FA has been clear with the independent consultants that the company will never directly compete with them for sales.

The clothing is of premium quality and is priced at a premium amount. The top-selling products include hooded sweatshirts and workout tops, pants, and shorts. Other items that broaden the product range include items such as water bottles, body wash, and running shoes.

A typical customer of FA is a woman between the ages of 25 and 45. She loves to be outdoors and loves to exercise. Being healthy is important to her and she is at peace with herself. She has always felt the need to belong in group settings and loves to shop.

All clothing is priced at total cost plus 60%. The pricing is very high and makes the products "exclusive." Not everyone can afford to be part of the FA "club." No item ever goes on sale. If a product doesn't sell, it goes to waste.

The two sisters have attributed their success to finding a way to make people feel good about themselves. If something makes a person feel good, they are often willing to pay more money. The FA manufacturing plant currently has capacity to use about 5 million machine hours. It is currently using about 3 million machine hours.

FA has been approached by a well-recognized national charity that supports women's health. The charity has asked FA to manufacture 1 million cycling jerseys for its annual cycling event. The event requires each participant to raise $2,000 in order to be eligible to ride their bike from one destination to another. Each participant must also purchase the cycling jersey. The charity has suggested that each participant will pay $30 for a jersey. This represents a fraction of the retail selling price of $75 (see Exhibit 1). Although FA currently manufactures cycling jerseys, the sisters are not sure if they should accept this offer. In order to manufacture the jerseys, FA would have to purchase a screen print machine that would cost $200,000 and incur $25,000 of set-up costs. Because of the screen printing, these custom jerseys would require an additional 0.25 labour hours and 0.5 machine hours each.

Required

The sisters decided they needed the help of an expert and have engaged you, a professional accountant, for advice. They have provided you with the current cost to manufacture a similar jersey (Exhibit 1). They have asked you to prepare a report that outlines whether or not they should accept this one-time order. They would like you to consider both qualitative and quantitative factors. Prepare the report for the owners of FA.

EXHIBIT 1 – CYCLING JERSEY COST INFORMATION (PER JERSEY, BASED ON 4 MILLION JERSEYS PRODUCED ANNUALLY)

Material	$10.46
Direct labour: 0.5 hours @$12.15 per hour	$6.08
Overhead—Variable: 0.75 machine hours @$7.10 per hour	$5.33
Overhead—Fixed per jersey	$7.00
Total costs	**$28.87**
Markup	$46.18
Selling price	**$75.00**

Chapter 13: Capital Budgeting

13.1 ForeverTurf Inc.

ForeverTurf Inc. (FTI) is a manufacturer of artificial turf for sport, landscape, and playground applications. FTI is divided into three main divisions—Sport, Landscape, and Playground—and each division is treated as a profit centre. FTI's strategy is to deliver the most dynamic and innovative range of artificial turf surfaces, meeting the highest performance standards and producing customized solutions for a wide range of customers.

Ryan Rumley, the newly appointed VP of Accounting for the Sport Division, looks out his office window and considers an e-mail about a new machine that has just been developed. The new machine is an upgraded version of FTI's existing machine, used to manufacture the company's artificial turf for soccer fields. Ryan is not sure if it makes sense to buy this new machine, since the old machine was purchased only two years ago. However, the annual cost savings proposed by the manufacturer of the new machine seem attractive. Ryan is especially interested in investigating this new machine because his annual bonus is tied to FTI's net income, so any cost reductions will benefit him personally as well as the company.

The initial cost of the new machine is $200,000 and it has a useful life of seven years. There is also an initial set-up cost of $7,000, which is required to integrate the new machine with FTI's existing equipment. At the end of seven years, the machine is expected to have a salvage value of $24,000.

Ryan knows he has to accurately estimate the annual cost savings from the new machine. The new machine is more automated than the existing machine, which will result in savings of 2,000 direct labour hours each year. The labour rate is $16 per hour. Ryan knows that the new machine will likely be more expensive to run and he estimates increased power and maintenance costs of $250 per month. The existing machine has a contribution margin of $330 per unit.

Another benefit Ryan envisions relates to the company's product line and customer base. Currently, FTI's artificial turf is sold primarily to local schools, universities, and soccer clubs. Major League Soccer recently announced plans to sponsor a professional soccer club in a major city only 100 km from FTI. Professional soccer fields require a slightly higher grade of turf, but the production process is very similar to that for the type of turf FTI currently produces. The professional turf could only be produced with the new machine Ryan is considering. FTI's existing machine cannot produce professional-grade turf.

FTI currently has available capacity to produce professional-grade turf in addition to its regular turf. It would cost FTI $0.50 per square metre to supply the turf for a professional field, and 7,000 square metres would be needed. Ryan estimates the sales price of the professional turf at $50,000 and believes that this sale would take place in two years.

Ryan knows the new machine is good strategically for FTI, and he expects more professional soccer fields to be built in the future as professional soccer gains popularity. But he's not sure if it makes sense to replace a machine that was bought only two years ago. FTI paid $100,000 to buy the existing machine and is depreciating it on a straight-line basis over its estimated useful life. The existing machine's book value is $60,000 and FTI could sell it today for $25,000 and recognize a $35,000 loss.

Before Ryan prepares his report to the division's senior management, he reconsiders the estimated labour hour savings. He wonders how the analysis would change if the labour hour savings was increased by 10%. This estimate could have a significant impact on the final decision because it is an annual number. Ryan is a big soccer fan and wants to see FTI expand the business to professional fields, but to do that they need the new machine. He knows the 2,000 hours was a reasonable estimate provided by the operations department, but he decides to increase it by 10% in his analysis to make sure the new machine is purchased. After all, how do they really know how much time will be saved until they have the new machine operating?

FTI has a required rate of return of 12% for all capital investments.

Required

Prepare the report that Ryan would submit to the Sport division's senior management recommending whether FTI should purchase the machine to make professional-grade turf. Round your calculations to the nearest dollar.

13.2 Chickadee Ski Club

Chickadee Ski Club (CSC) is located in southern Ontario near large urban centres but not far enough north to guarantee a full winter of snow on the ground. The club's revenue and profit jump in years when the weather is cold and snowy but fall when the winters are mild. When the club was founded 30 years ago, winters in southern Ontario were consistently cold and there was snow on the ground from mid-November until early spring, approximately four months of business for a ski hill. Now, winters are much more unpredictable and CSC is considering ways it can adapt to the changing climate to remain profitable and offer skiers a fantastic ski experience.

CSC purchased its current snow-making equipment eight years ago. While the equipment still works, it has to be moved around the ski hill manually using sleds and the snow it produces is low quality.

CSC's operations manager, Louise Crépeau, is considering purchasing 40 new high-pressure snow guns. The new snow guns are permanently attached to poles in various places on the ski hills, eliminating the need to move the equipment around the ski hill. The snow guns produce higher-quality snow and, most importantly, they can be used at a warmer temperature than the old snow-making equipment. Louise estimates the high-pressure snow guns will extend CSC's season approximately two weeks since it can make snow when the weather is warmer.

The following information relates to the purchase of the new snow guns:

» CSC wants to buy 40 high-pressure snow guns at $5,000 each. The new snow guns are expected to last five years and have an estimated salvage value of $250 each.

» CSC can sell its current snow-making equipment for $4,000 today.

» If Louise buys the new snow guns, she will no longer need an employee to move the old snow-making equipment around the ski hill. Assume this person works for 3 months of the year, 10 days per month, and 6 hours per day. The labour rate for this type of worker is $15 per hour.

» The new snow guns also use less electricity. Louise estimates they will save $100 per month during the three months of the year they are open for business.

» Since the new snow guns can make snow when the weather is warmer, Louise believes this will extend their ski season by at least two weeks (most likely one week earlier at the beginning of the season and one week later at the end of the season). The price of a lift ticket is $50, approximately 300 skiers use the hill on a typical day, and CSC's contribution margin percentage is 20%.

Chickadee Ski Club has a required rate of return of 10% for all capital investments.

Required

You have been hired as an outside consultant to write a report for CSC recommending whether it should buy the snow guns. Your report should analyze the relevant quantitative and qualitative aspects of the decision and also consider any issues that will impact the decision. Round your calculations to the nearest dollar.

13.3 Golf Incorporated

Contributed by
Jo-Anne Ryan CPA, CA, PhD
Assistant Professor, Laurentian University, Barrie

Golf Inc. (GI) operates a thriving golf cart delivery business, delivering golf carts to golf courses throughout the world on behalf of the cart manufacturers. With gas prices climbing at an alarming rate, the owner of GI, Forest Podrasky, is contemplating opening up a distribution centre in Canada to complement his centre in England. GI's revenue comes from the royalties paid by companies, such as Club Cart, whenever GI delivers golf carts to the businesses. Expenses include utilities, salaries to the delivery personnel, and other expenses. Exhibit 1 provides details of the proposed new centre in Canada.

You are a consultant who specializes in project evaluations and have been hired by GI. Forest would like you to prepare a report to him that analyzes the quantitative information provided in Exhibit 1. In addition to your quantitative analysis, Forest would like you to include in the memo a discussion of any limitations you noted.

Finally, he is relying on you to discuss any other risks that he should be aware of if he goes ahead with this venture.

Required

Prepare the report for Forest.

EXHIBIT 1 – CANADIAN DISTRIBUTION CENTRE DETAILS

Details for the distribution costs are:

» Your consultant's fee for providing this analysis is $30,000.

» Forest expects that this Canadian venture will end in eight years.

» The distribution centre will be leased in Canada by GI at a cost of $80,000 per year.

» Revenues are expected to be as follows: Years 1 to 5 an increase of $310,000 each year, year 6 $330,000, year 7 $290,000, and year 8 $280,000.

» A plane will be purchased just for this distribution centre (it will not be purchased if the Canadian venture does not proceed). The cost of the plane is $1.8 million. The salvage value at the end of year 8 is expected to be $120,000.

» Increased salaries for the new centre are expected to be $60,000 per year for each of the eight years.

» Utilities are expected to be 15% of yearly revenues.

» GI expects an additional working capital requirement of $250,000 at the beginning. This amount will be recovered at the end of year 8.

» The tax rate for GI is 40% and the capital cost allowance rate on the plane is 20%. GI's discount rate is 10%.

» The 12 workers who would have to move from England are not happy about the centre being in Canada as Canada's football is not the same as theirs. GI has offered to pay them a one-time bonus of $15,000 (shared among all the workers), payable at the end of year 6.

» At the end of the contract, GI will receive a completion bonus of $4,000,000.

13.4 Summertime Golf Ltd.

Contributed by
Jo-Anne Ryan CPA, CA, PhD
Assistant Professor, Laurentian University, Barrie

Summertime Golf Ltd. (SGL) was founded by Mike Borrelli on January 1, 20X1. SGL is a small private corporation selling golf equipment in the Winnipeg area. Mike is the majority shareholder. Mike's cousin Vinny owns some of the common shares after purchasing them this year and would like to be an active member of the company.

Mike has hired you as a management consultant as he is trying to determine his next course of action. Recently the business next to SGL closed, and there is approximately 3,000 square feet (275 square metres) of space available to him if he wishes to rent it. Mike doesn't quite know what he should do but he believes that this is the perfect opportunity to expand his business and take advantage of the growing golf industry. He is considering renting the space and installing two virtual golf simulators and will call the business Big Mike's Virtual Golf (BMVG). Mike believes that he can capitalize on the popularity of virtual golf and that it would also help his golf store as customers would move back and forth between both locations. Financial details of SGL can be found in Exhibit 1.

Mike is in a relatively stable financial position but doesn't want to get too far into debt by jumping into new ventures that don't look like they will benefit him. He really needs you to look at the proposal and provide an analysis including the pricing strategy and any other issues you can identify.

Mike copied the quote from the manufacturer of the golf simulator, Full Swing Golf, and included it as Exhibit 2. It details the costs of the acquisition and installation of the simulators along with ongoing costs. Other operational costs are contained in Exhibit 1.

Mike leaves your office and you begin to prepare your report for him. You realize that you will need to make some assumptions on your numbers and that there are both quantitative and qualitative implications. You told Mike that you would start by preparing a net present value analysis.

Required

Prepare the report to Mike with your analysis of the proposal to start BMVG.

EXHIBIT 1 – SGL YEAR-TO-DATE HIGHLIGHTS

» Currently SGL has a capital structure that is 50% debt and 50% equity financing. The company's current cost of debt is 2% above the prime lending rate (prime is currently 2.5%). The company's cost of equity is estimated to be 20%. SGL is currently paying income taxes at the marginal rate of 37%. (Note: round your percentage to the nearest whole percent.)

» SGL must lease the entire 3,000 square feet; renting a smaller portion is not possible. The annual price per square foot is $22 and the landlord is also asking for 1% of revenues to be paid on an annual basis under a five-year contract. The simulators and related bar space would use approximately 2,000 square feet. The landlord would pay for all the renovation costs except for a one-time fee of $6,000 payable by Mike Borrelli immediately (assume these are non-depreciable costs). Currently Mike believes the 1,000-square-foot unused space will be used as storage.

» Mike has already paid $2,000 for a consultant to discuss the possibility (although she provided no calculations).

» The capital cost allowance rate for this type of equipment would be 20%.

» There are approximately 400,000 potential customers within a driving radius of BMVG. Each virtual game simulator costs between $12 and $15 per person for a half-hour session and can accommodate groups of up to 12. Mike intends to operate the business between 11 a.m. and 9 p.m. each day, seven days per week. Most of the customer traffic is expected between 5 and 9 p.m. Full Swing Golf provided data that suggest that the maximum occupancy at any time is 24 (12 players per simulator) and that you can expect, on average, two spectators for each player. Between 11 a.m. and 5 p.m., you can expect, on average, about 50% full capacity (of players) throughout the life of the simulator. For the busy period between 5 and 9 p.m., you can expect 100% capacity for the first year, 80% for year 2, and 75% for years 3, 4, and 5. The simulators have a five-year life and a salvage value of $2,000 each.

» Mike would be responsible for other one-time costs for dishes, glasses, and other equipment for the bar as well as upfront consumables. (Assume these are all part of working capital requirements.) This amounts to $50,000 and will be returned at the end of the five years.

» There will be two servers and two cooks working at any one time. Each employee will be paid $13 per hour, with hours being calculated as opening time plus a half hour prior to opening and a half hour after opening. The $13 is expected to increase by 3% per year. Assume this includes all government remittances and deductions.

» Restaurant revenues are estimated to average $10,000 per month over the five-year period, with cost of sales averaging 47% (excluding salaries, which are calculated separately).

» A golf simulator is a computer-generated program with sensors to simulate a real golf game. The simulator is preloaded with famous golf courses from around the world (for example, St. Andrews, Augusta, and Bethpage). Customers bring in and use their own golf clubs and golf balls.

EXHIBIT 2 – SIMULATOR QUOTE

Quote

Full Swing Golf

21 Anywhere Road
Somewhere, Ontario, L1N 7A3   **DATE: August**
Phone 705-555-5555

Quote For: **For:**
Mike Borrelli   Golf Simulators
Summertime Golf Inc.

DESCRIPTION	AMOUNT

Quote #: 459870
Client: Summertime Golf Ltd.
 	
Equipment:
2 Deluxe Virtual Golf Machines including:
  - Computers
  - Software
  - Projection screens
  - HD projector
  - 15 golf courses plus practice green
  - Touchscreen
  - Branded awning
  - Enclosure
    $425,000 each
	$850,000

Installation: Installation extra and includes a one-year on-site warranty	10,000
Updates: Annual fee to cover software updates and technical questions	2,000
Bonus: 10 hours of free training for your staff ******* All Amounts subject to HST *******	
	$862,000